Hamlyn
London · New York · Sydney · Toronto

VIC WILLOUGHBY

Acknowledgments

The author is grateful to Victor Horsman
for providing many oldtimers' Christian
names, which are more in keeping with the
friendly spirit of motor cycling than are
initials.

The publishers are grateful to the editor of
Motor Cycle for permission to reproduce the
majority of illustrations in this book, and
also to: Associated Press; BMW; Gilera;
Bob Green; the late John Griffith and the
Stanford Hall museum; W. Gruder;
International News Photos; Keystone;
Dr Helmut Krackowizer; C.V. Middleton;
the National Motor Museum; Nick
Nicholls; NSU; Ken Price; Publifoto;
Salmond Photography; Norman Sharpe;
Sport and General; J. Stoddart; David
Burgess Wise; Mick Woollett; K. Wörner.

Published by the Hamlyn Publishing Group Limited
London · New York · Sydney · Toronto
Astronaut House, Feltham, Middlesex, England
Copyright © The Hamlyn Publishing Group Limited, 1975
Second Impression 1976

ISBN 0 600 31870 2

Filmset by Keyspools Limited, Golborne, Lancashire
Printed in Great Britain by Alabaster Passmore Limited

Contents

Introduction

So profusely is motor-cycle history studded with fascinating designs that the basic difficulty in compiling this book was not which machines to include, but which to leave out.

Restricting the contents to roadsters and road racers helped solve the problem, though the most exciting designs in other branches of the sport–such as speed records, drag racing and so on–have no less claim to fame. Even in the context of road and road-racing machines, enthusiasts will never be unanimous as to which designs have the most merit. For motor cycling engenders such strong loyalties and enthusiasms that any judgement must be subjective.

We may all be proud, however, that the best motor-cycle designs have long been regarded as a yardstick of efficiency by engineers in other automotive fields. There is no substitute for brains, and motor cycling has never lacked its fair share.

The 40 machines covered here show a

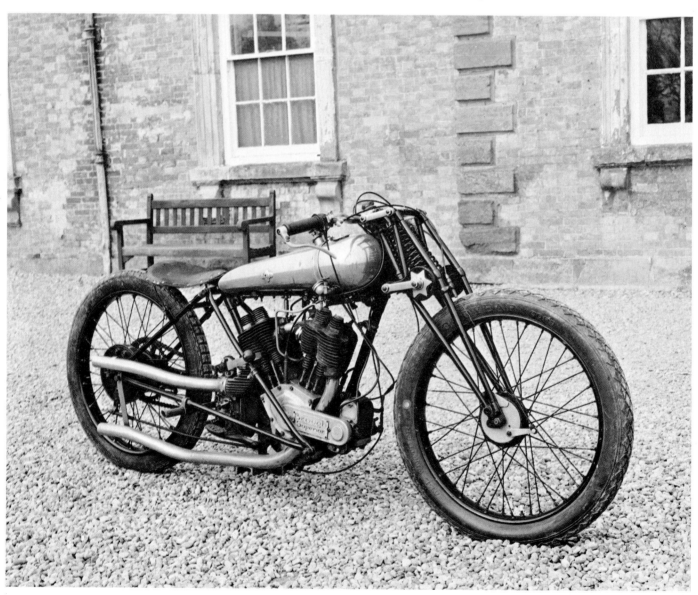

tremendous variety of ideas, and should provide something for every enthusiast, whether his personal preference is for the old or new, large or small, simple or complex, two-stroke or four-stroke, single or multi.

No single criterion has been used to determine which machines are classics. The Triumph twin is included largely for its commercial success; the desmodromic Ducati for its audacity; the Velocette Roarer for its enterprise; the Gilera four as a trendsetter; the Ariel Square Four for its individuality; the Moto-Guzzi single for its inspiration; the Brough Superior Dream for its technical novelty–and so on.

Some chapters cover more than one model, where there is a common theme or other similarity.

One thing is common to every model. They are all milestones along the path of progress.

V.H.W.

Left *reconditioned Velocette Roarer, which has the exhaust air deflectors missing*

Opposite page *'Old Bill', George Brough's personal side-valve racer and forerunner of the SS80*

7

Zenith Gradua

Single gears were all very well for steam loco-motives. Watching from a mainline plat-form, many an early motor-cycle designer must have envied his locomotive counterpart as the highly polished piston rods were rammed slowly but relentlessly out of their massive cylinders, hauling hundreds of tons off the mark on the same direct gearing that was good for 100mph and more way up the track.

This could never be with petrol engines, especially the motor-cycle variety, with their relatively small capacity and high perform-ance. Their best torque and power are restricted to comparatively narrow bands of revs, and a gearbox providing several over-all ratios is essential to cope with the range of

conditions from uphill restart to flat-out blind.

But engines were invented before gear-boxes, and although the small-bore ports, modest valve timings and low compression ratios of the early machines made them extremely tractable, their single gear ratios set severe limits to their overall performance.

In early machines, drive was usually by a vee-belt running directly from a pulley on the crankshaft to another on the rear wheel. The first move towards variable gearing was the adjustable engine pulley. Within limits, the outer flange of the pulley could be moved along the shaft. Obviously, when it was closest to the fixed flange the effective dia-meter of the pulley was largest and the gear

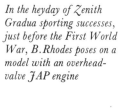

In the heyday of Zenith Gradua sporting successes, just before the First World War, B.Rhodes poses on a model with an overhead-valve JAP engine

ratio highest. When the flange was moved out to the other limit, the effective diameter of the pulley was smallest and the ratio lowest. Clearly, if the belt was correctly tensioned for the high gear, it was hopelessly slack for the low one, and trials riders carried two belts of different lengths, one for each gear.

In such events as the Auto-Cycle Union Six Days Trial (forerunner of the Scottish) riders would stop at the foot of each observed hill, wind the pulley flange out to give the low gear, and fit the shorter belt. They would then storm the hill flat out, relying on prior tuning of the engine to withstand any over-revving. With the summit safely reached, the longer belt would be refitted and the flange wound in again for high gear. The snag with this ruse was that it was practicable only by virtue of lax time schedules.

The Zenith Gradua gear, which could be varied widely without stopping the machine, provided the breakthrough.

Invented in 1908 by Freddie Barnes, Zenith's ace designer, it was controlled from the saddle by a 'coffee-grinder' handle at the top of a vertical shaft on the right-hand side of the engine, alongside the carburettor. The bottom of the shaft was connected to both the engine pulley and the rear-wheel spindle. Turning the handle one way expanded the pulley flanges by means of a quick-pitch thread (to lower the gear ratio) while simultaneously moving the wheel back in slotted fork lugs to keep the belt correctly tensioned. Winding the handle back brought the flanges closer together (so raising the

gear) and moved the wheel forward to suit.

For ordinary road work the Gradua gear was an enormous advance on fixed gearing. A *Motor Cycle* test, quoting a range from 9:1 (bottom) to 3½:1 (top), found the Zenith would restart and accelerate up London's Muswell Hill (1 in 9), then romp down a 1-in-12 slope without over-revving.

Yet the real pay-off was in competitions, especially in hill climbs. While their opponents had to make do with one ratio (the engine slogging or over-revving with variations in the gradient) Zenith riders just tweaked the handle as necessary and beat them time and again.

In 1911, Barnes won 53 hill climbs. And, although countershaft gearboxes were in vogue by the following year, he then improved his score to 58. Indeed, the Zenith Gradua became so dominant that the ACU barred it from single-gear events. Which was a boon rather than a blow to the makers, for they proudly exploited the word 'barred' as a trademark.

For all that, the Gradua gear had its limitations. Nothing less than a beefy big-twin engine could really do justice to the top gear on level going. And belt slip set in at about 6½:1, becoming chronic in rain.

There was the added snag that the efficiency of the rear brake varied considerably with wheel position.

It would be two or three years before countershaft gears really took over, with chain primary drive and chain or belt final drive. Meanwhile, the Zenith Gradua was superseded by the Rudge Multi, designed in

Above *a vee-twin version of the Zenith Gradua, with pulley control handle on the left*

Right *vintage Douglas racing twin, with gearbox over the rear cylinder*

Footboards indentify this as a roadster version of the 1912 Indian vee-twin, with inlet-over-exhaust valves

In this variant, the adjustable belt pulley is not on the crankshaft, but chain driven in front of the crankcase. Note the bevel gearing at the bottom of the control shaft

A 1920 5hp side-valve model. As in the other illustrations, the 'coffee-grinder' handle is on the left side, not the right, where it was in the original layout

the incredibly brief span of ten days for the 1911 Senior TT.

In this layout, with control by a side lever, the effective diameters of both pulleys varied together, the one expanding as the other contracted, and vice versa. Hence belt tension was automatically maintained without the need to move the rear wheel, and brake efficiency was constant.

The gearing range was much the same, with top something of an overdrive and bottom encouraging belt slip. But although the Multi was an improvement on the Gradua, belt problems eventually proved fatal to all such devices, including the Philipson pulley.

Their death was gradual rather than sudden, however. They were cheap, quiet, smooth and light, and riders were familiar with them. Chains were at first suspected of being dearer, noisier, harsher, heavier–and untried.

But there was no denying progress–and countershaft gearboxes, with chain primary and secondary drives, have now been with us for more than 60 years.

Indian vee-twin

Stagnation was indelibly scrawled across the face of the American motor-cycle industry in the early 1920s, by the advent of the ultra-cheap, mass-produced car. So it seems unbelievable that the industry was not only buoyant before the First World War, but in the very vanguard of technical progress.

Way back in 1904, while European riders fiddled with throttle levers, their transatlantic cousins on Indians had twistgrips. Only four years later, Indian had switched to mechanical inlet valves, though suction operation was still common in Europe. In 1914, the year the war started, acetylene lighting was still usual east of the Atlantic (and, in an emergency, many a rider used the contents of his bladder to keep the lamp burning!). But that year Indians not only had electric lighting, they had electric starting, too, nearly half a century before it was made commonplace by the Japanese manufacturers.

Indian's apparently rosy prospects were typical of the whole American industry.

Yet, scarcely was the war forgotten than the number of American manufacturers had dwindled to two – Indian and Harley-Davidson. And most of their production was for speed cops, so effectively had the cheap car swamped the transport market. From then on, European enthusiasts – with a wide choice of light, lithe, sporting models – pitied their Yankee cousins, with little choice but heavy, clumsy, woolly vee-twins.

It was, then, in the decade preceding the First World War that the American industry's star shone brightest – and never brighter than in the 1911 Senior TT in the Isle of Man.

Ask a TT fan which was the first make of machine to score a 1–2–3 in the TT? Not Rudge in the 1930 Junior, but Indian 19 years earlier. Or the first foreign bike to humiliate the British industry by winning a Senior? No, not Stanley Woods' 120-degree, vee-twin Moto-Guzzi in 1935, but Oliver Godfrey's 585cc Indian vee-twin way back in 1911.

This forerunner of the phenomenally successful 1911 racing twins has pedalling gear and an unsprung front fork. It is on Daytona Beach, with A.G.Chapple aboard.

Following pages *a reconditioned oval-tank Scott water-cooled twin*

13

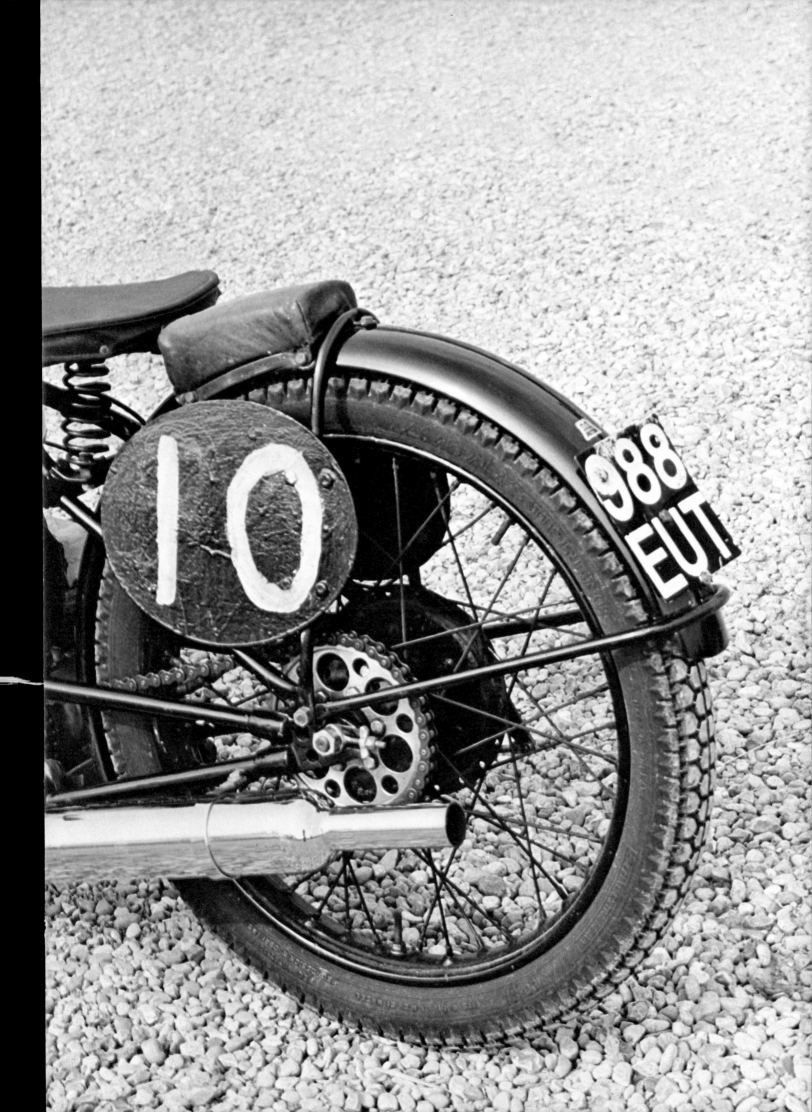

That year was as important a milestone in TT history as it was in Indian history. After four years on the comparatively flat, 15·8-mile St John's circuit, the races were shifted to the world's most famous and exacting lap – the 37¾-mile Mountain course – to test engines to the hilt. Pedalling gear was forbidden, and every machine had to struggle over Snaefell five times under its own power if it was even to finish.

For the first time, the programme was divided into Senior and Junior events. Yet there was a queer anomaly in the regulations governing engine capacities: twins were allowed larger engines than singles. While Senior singles were restricted to 500cc, twins were allowed 585cc because they were reckoned unreliable and less efficient, despite flat-out Brooklands tests which had shown the extra capacity to be worth from four to five miles in each hour.

True, the 1911 TT bonus was the smallest ever for the twins, for it had been whittled down year by year. But then, as now, it made no sense technically. For the brilliant Dr Fred Lanchester had already explained how stepping up the number of cylinders in an engine also steps up its potential power, though not in direct proportion. Indeed, Lanchester's calculations are the basis for Jack Williams' proposed formula for scaling

down the capacity allowance with increase in cylinders, so as to give all types of engine the same power potential.

Pity the poor two-strokes, though. In 1911 they were considered to have such an unfair advantage that their actual capacity was multiplied by 1·25 for entry purposes, or 1·32 in the case of the water-cooled Scott twins.

When George Hendee and designer Oscar Hedstrom started making Indians in Springfield, Massachusetts, in 1900 they settled on the unusual layout of a rear-sloping (1¾hp) engine doing duty as a saddle tube, rather like a back-to-front Panther. The first major change was inevitable: adding a forward-sloping cylinder and so making a 3½hp vee-twin.

That occurred in 1905, and the model grew through 5 to 7hp.

Especially for the 1911 Senior TT, they scaled the engine down to 3¾hp (70 × 76mm × 2 = 585cc) and built a batch of bright-red racers, with chain drive and the two-speed countershaft gearbox previously available only on the 7hp model. Overall gearing was 3·5 to 1 (top) and 5·08 to 1 (bottom).

To accommodate the gearbox in the short wheelbase, the flywheels and crankcase were reduced in diameter. Standard Indian features included overhead inlet and side

Oliver Godfrey crosses the line to win the first Isle of Man Senior TT to be run on the 37¾-mile Mountain course. The race was over five laps, and Indians also filled the next two places

exhaust valves, mechanical oiling and detachable cylinder heads.

On the racers, however, the heads were secured by three bolts, not four, while the gear control was moved forward, close to the handlebar, so it could be operated from a crouch. Since the standard footboards were abandoned in favour of pegs, the rocking clutch pedal on the right was also discarded. Instead, a hand lever alongside the two-gallon tank could be set in any position to give the required degree of slip. Both brakes were foot controlled.

An extra oil tank was installed behind the seat tube, with an adjustable drip feed to the gearbox. Incidentally, the front fork was leaf sprung, and both handlebar grips twisted – the left one for the throttle, the right for both ignition advance and valve lifting.

The week's record entry of 104 was double that in 1910. Of the 64 Senior machines, 24 were twins and the Indians, backed by UK importer Billy Wells, were strongly tipped. No wonder. Oliver Godfrey, their star rider – small, athletic, plucky and experienced – had smashed the single-cylinder hour record at Brooklands only four months earlier. And American champion Jake de Rosier came over with a tremendous reputation, after shattering all records from 1 to 100 miles four months before Godfrey's Brooklands triumph.

Besides them, there were Charlie Franklin, Arthur Moorhouse and Jimmy Alexander, all among the very cream of road racers. And well the Indian team knew that their most formidable rivals were Charlie Collier, on a Matchless-JAP single, and Frank Philipp, who anticipated both sartorial and technical fashions by half a century – he wore purple leathers, to match the colour of his Scott twin, and the engine had rotary inlet valves.

For the first time in the TT, silencers, though still compulsory for practising, could be left off for the race. And, some three-quarters of an hour after the start, de Rosier roared throatily into his second lap, with a lead of more than half a minute on Godfrey, who had needed a long push to get started, and Collier. Moorhouse was fourth, Franklin sixth.

De Rosier's pace was too good to last. And, as the American slowed on the second lap,

Runner-up to Godfrey in the 1911 Senior TT was Charlie Franklin, who steadily worked his way up from sixth on the opening lap

Collier delighted the home industry by taking a commanding lead. Godfrey lay third, slowed by his one and only fuel stop, and Moorhouse moved to fifth in support of Franklin. At Willaston, Alexander came a cropper, gashing a knee and damaging the right-hand twistgrip.

By the end of lap three, Collier's lead was nearly a minute, and Godfrey had moved ahead of de Rosier. Philipp's Scott howled through to claim the day's fastest lap, in 44min 52sec. But he was nowhere in the running, and Franklin and Moorhouse kept their positions. With the race more than half run, four Indians were led by the solitary Matchless.

Then, on lap four, the leader board went haywire. Collier punctured and dropped to third. De Rosier spent a disastrous 20 minutes in Ramsey, fiddling with the rear inlet valve and sparking plug. And Godfrey stepped up the pace to take a two-minute lead over Franklin. Moorhouse plodded on, now fourth.

But the real excitement was saved for the final lap. While Godfrey gave the engine a precautionary squirt of oil from the auxiliary pump as he started the mountain climb, Collier rode like a demon, bested Franklin, and halved Godfrey's lead. In his haste, though, the Matchless star had refuelled away from the official depots in Douglas and Ramsey – and he was disqualified, leaving Franklin and Moorhouse to complete the Indian 1–2–3.

De Rosier finished a plucky 11th. But he, too, was ruled out – for fitting a nut and a plug not carried on the machine!

The arduous Mountain course had taught its first lessons. As far as the manufacturers were concerned, the single-speed racer was clearly finished, as was the three-speed hub gear with direct belt drive. Chain drive and countershaft gearboxes were here to stay. For the organisers, the lesson was that a capacity bonus for multis was grossly unfair. There was a suggestion of giving singles a bonus, instead. But, for 1912, the present flat capacity limits of 500cc for the Senior TT and 350cc for the Junior were introduced.

The silencer identifies this as a road-going version of the 1911 Indian two-speed vee-twin. Valve arrangement was inlet over exhaust, and throttle control by twistgrip

Scott

Probably the best-loved Scotts were the Squirrels, Super Squirrels and Flying Squirrels of the 1920s and 1930s – fascinating, purple, water-cooled two-stroke twins of 500cc and 600cc that established a cult of almost religious fervour. But the sheer genius of Alfred Angas Scott lay much deeper and went back much farther. Indeed, he left the company in 1919 (to concentrate on an unorthodox three-wheeler) and died of pleurisy in 1923.

Scott had an uncanny flair for combining highly original ideas with sound, practical engineering. Such was the range of his vision that not only were the basic features of his design practically unchanged throughout the marque's production, but he anticipated technical trends by up to half a century.

One of the mainstays of present-day Japanese two-stroke production – and as charming an engine type as any – the 180-degree parallel twin was Scott's choice way back at the turn of the century, when he put an experimental unit in a pushbike frame. Even today, water cooling of such an engine is something of a racing sophistication. Yet Scott engines had water-cooled heads from the very beginning, then rang the changes between cylinders and heads for a time, and were completely water cooled from 1914 onward.

Rotary inlet valves provided a breakthrough for racing two-strokes in the late 1950s. Scott introduced them in the 1911 TT. Moreover, his valve — a cylindrical one – controlled the transfer phase as well as the inlet.

Now practically universal, telescopic front forks gained a tentative foothold shortly before the Second World War. Scott had them before the First World War, with the sliders cross-braced at the top and controlled

Frank Philipp, one of the earliest Scott stars, astride a 1910 air-cooled model. It had a duplex triangulated frame, telescopic front fork, stirrup front brake and saddle-tube tank

First Senior TT for the legendary Jimmy Simpson was the 1922 event, in which he rode a water-cooled Scott. Here, on Ramsey Promenade, he poses on team-mate Harry Langman's machine

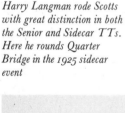

Harry Langman rode Scotts with great distinction in both the Senior and Sidecar TTs. Here he rounds Quarter Bridge in the 1925 sidecar event

by a central spring unit. He was alive, too, to the importance of frame stiffness and the lowest possible centre of gravity. And the legendary roadholding of his machines owed as much to the duplex, triangulated, straight-tube open frame – in which the engine was an integral, low-slung structural member – as to the fork action.

From the start of production in 1909 (when the Jowett car firm made the machines in Bradford, before his company set up independently at Saltaire, Yorks) Scott was one of the pioneers of all-chain drive and countershaft gears. Apart from the rocking-pedal foot control being about a quarter of a century ahead of its time, the

Scott two-speed gear was unique.

There were two primary drives, one each side of the central flywheel. Since the left and right sprockets were of different sizes, though on the same centres, they provided different gearing. Either of the driven sprockets could be locked to the counter-shaft (carrying the final-drive sprocket) by an internal, expanding-ring clutch controlled by the pedal. Rocking the pedal backward locked up the low-gear clutch, and forward the high gear. With the pedal horizontal both clutches were free for neutral.

Nor was Alfred Scott unaware of the rocking couple inherent in the 180-degree crankshaft. But he minimised the effect by putting plenty of weight in the rim of the large-diameter flywheel, and spacing the crankcase mountings as far apart as possible on the duplex frame tubes.

Incidentally, the use of overhung crank-pins with the central flywheel gave immediate access to the big ends on removal of covers from the crankcase sides.

Now that scientists are bitterly divided over the relative importance of heredity and early environment on human intelligence, Scott would make a fascinating study for them. He seems to have been blessed both ways – first as a member of a bright and extraordinarily large family, then on being

educated at Abbotsholme, where pupils were taught to think for themselves rather than meekly accept dogma.

It was in the summer of 1908 that the results of Scott's original thinking burst upon the sporting world. After winning a shield and gold medal at the Wass Bank hill-climb at the end of July, he took his smart little 333cc (58×63mm$\times 2$) machine to the year's most important climb – at Newnham, near Daventry – two weeks later, and trounced all comers with three of the most unobtrusive yet devastating ascents imaginable.

Bringing the engine to life by paddling effortlessly from the saddle while others ran-and-bumped, he zoomed invincibly up the hill – the smooth, catlike purr of the exhaust contrasting uncannily with the staccato bark of the four-strokes. Yet the little two-stroke's acceleration was so superior to that of its rivals that Scott scooped the twin-cylinder, variable-gear and open classes and three gold medals.

Everyone but he was dumbfounded. So much so that other manufacturers got together and bulldozed the Auto-Cycle Union into handicapping the Scott on the grounds that its extra firing impulses gave it an unfair advantage. For the following three years, the engine's actual capacity was multiplied by 1·32 for competition purposes.

The compliment was not lost on Alfred Scott, who promptly exploited it in his catalogue, even after the ban was lifted. Nor did the handicap diminish Scott successes. They continued to win hill-climbs against machines with larger engines. In 1910 a Scott was the first two-stroke ever to go the full distance in a TT (on the St John's circuit). And the following year Frank Philipp made the record lap in the Senior race (on the Mountain course) at 50·11mph.

That was the first year of the rotary valve, driven by chain from the crankshaft. Square ports in a double-ended sleeve connected the central carburettor with each crankcase in turn, after which additional ports provided a transfer passage from crankcase to cylinder. Ingeniously, the engine was not controlled by the usual throttle, but by a quick-thread device that advanced and retarded the whole timing of the valve.

It needed but little development to make the bike invincible in the 1912 Senior TT. Valve drive was changed to a train of gears, throttle control reinstated, compression ratio raised and each head fitted with a spare plug for emergency.

From start to finish of the race Frank

21

while leading early on, and it was left to Tim Wood – a member of the factory's repair staff riding in his first competition of any kind – to fill the breach.

Unfortunately, a six-minute stop at Braddan Bridge to tape up a leaking radiator connection put him down to 10th at the end of the opening lap, and he had to take on water every lap. But a record lap at 52·12 mph had him in the lead on lap three, and he eventually beat Ray Abbott (Rudge Multi) by a mere five seconds – with a nail embedded in his rear tyre.

When Wood shot into the lead in 1914 and pushed the lap record up to 53·5mph, Scott looked all set to be the first make to chalk up three Senior wins in a row. But Wood struck trouble and Rudge went on to notch their first TT victory, with a machine in the capable hands of Cyril Pullin.

Scott racing design changed little after the First World War, though a conventional two-speed gearbox, in conjunction with the double primary drive, gave four ratios, and the oval petrol tank under the saddle gave way to a wedge-shape tank filling the open frame. The factory never quite regained its pre-war dominance in the TT, but Harry Langman finished third in the 1922 Senior, set the lap record in the 1923 sidecar event and led until his last-lap crash at Braddan Bridge, then finished second in the 1924 Senior. The machines showed versatility, too, in winning the team prize in the tough ACU Six Days Trial in 1920.

Except for the rotary valve, Scott racers were substantially similar to the catalogue models. So it was no surprise that the Squirrel sports model, introduced in 1922, achieved a fanatical following, as did the Super Squirrel in 1925 and the super-tuned Flying Squirrel a year later. Subsequent variants on the theme included the Power-Plus TT Replica, the Sprint Special and the Speedway Special.

As the years rolled by, the twins bowed more and more to orthodoxy, with conventional three- and four-speed gearboxes, girder front forks and, on a short-lived six-fifty, a loop-type frame. But Alfred Scott's successors kept alive his spirit of originality when, just before the Second World War, they shook the industry with an experimental 1000cc three with a fore-and-aft crankshaft.

Alas, it was a victim of the years of conflict, and so the Scott reputation rests firmly on that wonderful succession of two-speeders that captured the hearts of connoisseurs for so many years.

Top with the exhaust belching blue smoke, Harry Langman accelerates away from Ballig Bridge in the wet 1928 Senior TT

Above the standard model, scheduled for 1940. By that time, the marque had bowed to convention in fitting a girder fork and foot-change gearbox

Applebee was unchallenged, beating Jack Haswell (Triumph) by nearly seven minutes, at 48·69mph, and making the best lap at 49·44mph. Indeed, Haswell's second place was by courtesy of a last-lap tyre failure on Frank Philipp's Scott, which dropped it to 11th place after it had been a comfortable second right from the start.

The only significant changes for the 1913 TT were increased port sizes and the simultaneous firing of the double plugs by a special magneto. But Applebee went out

Douglas

There are two ways to install a flat-twin engine – the smoothest-running type ever put in a motor cycle. You can set the cylinders across the frame, as BMW do, which gives you ideal cooling, fine accessibility, foot protection, a short wheelbase and a heaven-sent opportunity to integrate the gearbox with the engine and fit enclosed shaft drive, which needs no attention beyond rare and simple oil changes. On the debit side, the shaft drive is expensive and the valve covers are vulnerable in the event of a minor tumble.

The alternative is to set the cylinders in line with the frame, as Douglas did in their heyday. That way you can fit the conventional and less-expensive chain drive, there is no problem of engine vulnerability, and the centre of gravity can be even lower. Cylinder cooling is unequal, however, and it is difficult to avoid an ungainly wheelbase, especially if the gearbox is placed behind the engine, as it was in many Douglas machines.

By far the best solution to the last problem is to put the box above the rear cylinder – and that was the layout of the most memorable

of all Douglases – the SW5 and SW6 racers and the DT5 and DT6 dirt-trackers. These were based on the outstandingly fast TT models on which, in 1923, Manxman Tom Sheard won the atrociously wet Senior race, Jim Whalley made the fastest lap while leading early on, and Freddie Dixon won the newly-inaugurated sidecar event with a 600cc banking outfit, originally sketched out in chalk on the workshop floor.

Yet, obvious though that engine-gearbox layout seems, it was the opposite arrangement – a high-mounted engine with the gearbox under the rear cylinder – that the Bristol concern chose for many of their earlier racers, including the original version of the overhead-valve five-hundred in 1920.

Founded in 1907, the Douglas company was no stranger to competition successes, even before the First World War. In 1911, Eli Clark – riding a light side-valve three-fifty with the engine tucked high under the tank, and direct belt drive – broke the Land's End–John O'Groats record with a time of 39 hours 40 minutes.

The following year Bill Bashall won the

The first Douglas had the 350cc side-valve engine tucked high under the tank, direct belt drive and pedalling gear. A similar machine broke the Land's End–John O'Groats record in 1911

Manxman Tom Sheard after winning the very wet 1923 Senior TT. The three-speed gearbox has cross-over drive, while the British Research Association front brake is of disc type

wet Junior TT at 39.65mph, with team-mate Eddie Kickham turning the fastest lap at 41.76mph. Those 1912 racing models still had side valves. But the two-speed counter-shaft gearbox was supplemented by a double primary drive, so giving a choice of four overall ratios. This was done by fitting an engine sprocket on each side of the outside flywheel, and either of the driven sprockets could be locked to the countershaft by a foot-controlled dog clutch, while the two gears in the box were selected by hand.

Later that year, for the Spanish TT (which Douglas won), the system was refined to give six speeds, by having three pairs of pinions in the box. The following year, 1913, the factory sustained its reputation when Billy Newsome finished a close second in the Junior TT, after which Douglases took the first three places in the Spanish TT and fourth in the French GP, then *the* European classic.

Came the war, and the factory produced no fewer than 25000 army models. When peace returned, so great was the demand for a civilian version, besides the 600cc side-valve, that other ventures, including experiments with a rear-springing layout designed in 1913, had to be shelved.

Then, in 1920, the seeds of future glory were sown, with the introduction of overhead valves for racing, although the crazy layout

of gearbox under engine was initially a built-in handicap. For the first time, the cylinder heads were detachable, with the pushrod-operated valves inclined at 90 degrees to one another. There was a single Senspray carburettor. Because of the length of the T-shape induction tract, there was an exhaust-heated muff in the middle.

Bore and stroke were 68 × 68mm (a 350cc version had the same stroke and a 57mm bore), the crankshaft was solid and there was an ingenious system of wick lubrication for the rockers, from aluminium reservoirs spanning the tops of the spindles. The cast-iron pistons had webbed central small-end bosses for forked con-rod ends, and engine oiling was by hand pump. The three-speed gearbox gave a cross-over drive and there was a British Research Association disc front brake, in which a vee-section friction shoe was pressed radially against a bevelled hub flange.

The hoped-for successes were not achieved, and for 1921 there was a switch to light-alloy cylinder heads and four speeds. Even so, the only worthwhile achievement was second and third places in the French GP.

The outlook brightened in 1922, however, not so much by virtue of seventh place in the Senior TT as by Cyril Pullin's achievement

in officially bettering 100mph in Britain for the first time on a five-hundred (100·06mph over an electrically-timed half-mile).

In the winter of 1922–3 the penny finally dropped with the Douglas engineers. The frame was shortened, the engine lowered as far as possible and the gearbox (three-speed) switched from under to over the rear pot. Two carbs were fitted, breathing from a common pressure-balance box, with the intake at the rear and a vertical baffle separating the carburettor mouths. Eloquent of the low anti-knock rating of the petrol at that time was the compression ratio – a paltry 5:1. Each valve had three springs. The engine-shaft clutch had a floating steel plate sandwiched between two friction discs. In spite of the engine's smoothness, flexible petrol pipes were adopted. Under the crankcase was a five-pint aluminium oil container, feeding the engine via a small compartment in the fuel tank. The disc brake, now fitted to both wheels, had a friction-faced disc and ribbed aluminium shoe. With the frame tubes sweeping steeply downward from the steering head, the whole machine was sleek, low and graceful. Moreover, at 250lb, it was up to 50lb lighter than some of its rivals.

Considering the whole redesign and building had been squeezed into five months, with the TT bikes shipped to the Isle of Man untried, their success there was incredible. Not only did Whalley lead convincingly for three laps before one cylinder packed up and the bike failed to climb Creg Willey's Hill, and not only did Sheard then dominate the remainder of the race – but on several laps Douglases occupied the first four positions and others were not far behind.

Alfie Alexander's third place in the Junior was further encouragement. But the real highlight other than the Senior win was Freddie Dixon's victory in the very first Sidecar TT, after Harry Langman crashed his Scott at Braddan Bridge when leading on the last lap.

That was only the start of a star-studded era for the ohv racing Douglases. Whalley won the French GP. Dixon was third in the following year's Senior TT after splintering the lap record, as he did in the sidecar event. In 1925 he pushed the sidecar lap still higher, although the race was won by his team-mate Len Parker, with the banking mechanism locked up and the passenger doing the customary acrobatics instead.

By that time dry sump oiling had been adopted, as had self-servo brakes, with one long, flexible shoe occupying the complete circumference of the drum.

But it was with a brakeless model, having

Another 1923 TT-winning Douglas – Freddie Dixon's 600cc outfit with banking sidecar, controlled by the passenger through a lever

1925 600cc (68 × 82mm) racing engine, with flywheel clutch, rocker return springs and oil reservoirs at the top of the rocker spindles

One of many Douglas successes in Continental events: Rudolf Runtsch wins the 500cc Semmering Wanderpreis race for the third time in 1930

no left-side footrest and a knee-hook on the right, that Douglas were soon to achieve the pinnacle of their fame.

Dirt-track racing came to Britain towards the end of the decade. From the hotch-potch of makes that were originally used in the new sport, Douglas soon emerged supreme. Their light weight and acceleration gave them an edge in performance. Their ultra-low centre of gravity and long wheelbase made them the most spectacular bikes ever to throw up a spume of cinders.

With superstars such as Australia's im-

mortal Vic Huxley enthralling the crowds everywhere, Douglases swamped the major honours and the company reaped the reward by selling no fewer than 1300 speedway models in 1929.

In financial straits, the company ventured into transverse engine mounting in 1935 (with the 500cc shaft-drive Endeavour), 1946 (chain-driven, torsion-sprung three-fifty) and 1954 (banana-styled three-fifty Dragonfly). But by the 1950s the final curtain was falling and there was never a hope of reviving the glories of the 1920s.

ABC

British BMW fans with a strong streak of patriotism have long taken pride in the assumption that the world-famous German design was originally copied from Granville Bradshaw's 398cc transverse flat-twin ABC.

Certainly the ABC was marketed in 1920, three years before the first BMW, and there were several similarities in layout. It is true, too, that both machines were launched to employ aircraft factories that would otherwise have stood idle following the armistice in November 1918. But there were as many fundamental differences as there were similarities. And, while BMW fulfilled their bright promise, producing half-a-million top-quality machines in their first half-century, the ABC marque flared briefly and died when only 2000 bikes had been made.

Both machines had the cylinders set across a duplex-loop frame. But, while the first BMW kept engine width to a minimum by using side valves, Bradshaw specified overhead valves and tackled the problem of engine vulnerability in a tumble by spacing the frame loops farther apart. Both engines had integral gearboxes. But, whereas the BMW had three speeds and a simple hand change, the ABC had four speeds and a car-type H-gate for the lever.

Front springing in both cases was by a quarter-elliptic leaf spring, but the BMW had a trailing-link fork, the ABC a girder. While the BMW frame was unsprung, the ABC was the first with pivoted rear suspension, again leaf-sprung.

Although the BMW had a drum brake at the front, it had a dummy belt rim at the rear, while the ABC had drums in both wheels.

Some of these comparisons suggest the British design was the more advanced, but it missed out badly in transmission. BMW took the obvious opportunity of the fore-and-aft crankshaft to use a shaft and enclosed bevel gears for the final drive. Bradshaw, putting rear springing first, realised that shaft drive would involve universal joints and plumped for the conventional chain. A pair of bevels behind the gearbox turned the drive through 90 degrees to suit the final-drive sprocket.

For all that, the ABC design, which was hatched in a mere 11 days following the armistice, was a sensation. After four years of war, its boldness and originality captured

Extremely advanced and refined for its day (just after the First World War), the transverse flat-twin ABC weighed only 175 lb despite its luxury specification

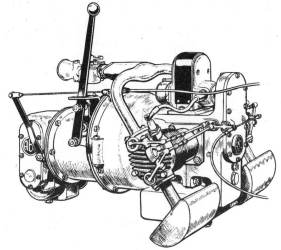

were aluminium diecastings with two rings above the gudgeon pin oil scraper below.

A great advance was single-lever control for the Claudel-Hobson carburettor, made possible by an exhaust-heated induction muff to promote vaporisation. Lubrication was wet sump, with the contents pumped round every three minutes at top speed, and there was a Rotherman visual oil-circulation indicator on the right-hand side of the crankcase. On top of the case sat the CAV magneto.

A cone-type clutch, controlled by a left-hand twistgrip, took the drive to the gearbox, which had ball and roller bearings for

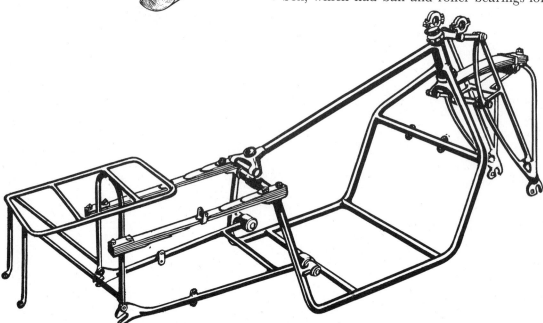

every imagination. It was not just another motor bike but a car on two wheels, with every detail thoroughly thought out.

Bradshaw was no newcomer to motorcycle design. Before the war, his All British (Engine) Company marketed conventional flat twins of 494cc (68 × 68mm), with the cylinders in line with the wheelbase. (The gearbox was behind the rear cylinder head, and the wheelbase was therefore ungainly. He was extraordinarily versatile, too, spawning – among other things – an airscrew-driven car, oil cooling for cylinders, and the 400hp Dragonfly aircraft engine with nine radial cylinders. Every ounce of his ingenuity was put into the post-war ABC.

First cousin of a War Office power unit for dynamos and blowers, the engine was way ahead of the general trend in having oversquare cylinders (68·6mm bore × 54mm stroke). Turned from steel billets, the very light cylinder barrels had six-bolt cast-iron heads with inclined, pushrod-operated valves and volute (spiral) springs. The pistons

the shafts, and gave overall ratios of 13·16, 9·75, 7·31 and 5·48 to 1. Drive for the dynamo was taken from the crown-wheel case behind the gearbox. After the usual disconnections, the whole power unit could be removed from the frame by undoing only four bolts.

Three cross-tubes spanned the frame's duplex loops. The rear fork, also crossbraced, was pivoted on two needle-roller bearings 10in apart. High alongside the wheel, each leaf spring was virtually two quarter-elliptics, joined at the thin end by having the longest leaf common to both.

A weathershield closed the front of the frame and had adjustable louvres for engine cooling. Inboard of the frame side tubes were footboards. There was a rubber cush-drive in the rear hub. Both wheels had knock-out spindles and bolt-on brake drums. All control cables were threaded through the handlebar.

Yet, notwithstanding the luxury specification, the ABC weighed only 175lb, which

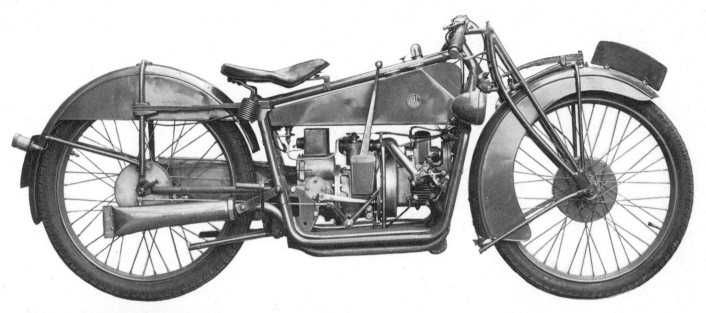

added a relatively brisk performance to its other attractions. In March, 1919, a *Motor Cycle* road test of an early prototype quoted a speed range of 10 to 60mph in top gear, snappy acceleration and fine hill climbing. The engine was smooth and quiet. And while the springing gave a comfortable floating sensation, the bike was very stable and refused to be provoked into a wobble.

Manufacture was entrusted to Sopwith, at Kingston-on-Thames, while Gnôme et Rhône were licensed to produce the machine in France. In no time at all the order books were bulging. But tooling and teething troubles caused delays, and the spring of 1919 came and went without the expected launch.

Hopes were revived in the autumn, when a modified machine was exhibited at Olympia. Gone was the sump and mechanical oiling. The oil was housed in the tank, with an adjustable sight-feed, worked by crankcase suction, and an auxiliary hand pump. The pushrods had been beefed up and their adjusters modified, tapered coil springs were fitted to the valves, and the dynamo had been

moved on to the top of the bevel box, driven by the gearbox mainshaft.

It was May 1920 before deliveries began. Meanwhile inflation had boosted the price to £160, and many who had not already cancelled their orders because of the delay did so on account of the price.

Tourists who stuck to their choice were charmed. Sportsmen found the bike fast enough to win speed trials. Jack Emerson broke the hour record twice at Brooklands during the year, first with 67·93 miles, then 70·44 miles. In the TT, ABC anticipated another fashion by using megaphone exhausts.

The loss of orders was followed by another blow. The flimsy valve gear proved too susceptible to over-revving, the kick starter was weak. There was no ABC at the 1920 London Show. The goodies trade marketed alternative rocker gear, with larger bearing surfaces and wick lubrication. But Britain's most promising design to that time faded away, before BMW launched *their* transverse flat twin on one of the most illustrious careers in motor-cycle history.

Ner-a-Car

Myth or fact? Was the Ner-a-Car really the safest and most stable of all solos, as many old-timers claimed? Or were they looking back some 30 years through rose-tinted spectacles? That was the issue I sought to settle one bitter-cold and snowy day early in 1954 when I borrowed a well-preserved 1925 Model C, with Blackburne 350cc side-valve engine, Sturmey Archer three-speed gearbox and, of course, hub-centre steering.

The name Ner-a-Car was extraordinarily apt. Not so much because it was a play on the American designer's name – Carl Neracher – but simply because no motor-cycle design could have stuck closer to car principles.

The frame was an ultra-low flat chassis, comprising two channel-section pressed-steel side members, cross-braced front and rear. At the front was pivoted a coil-sprung, U-shape axle, closed end forward, with an inclined kingpin fixed in the middle. A swivel arm on the hub was connected by a drag kink to a 20-per-cent-longer arm at the bottom of the vertical steering column, and the chassis side members were widely bowed out at the front to provide steering lock.

Except for the cylinder and head, the engine and gearbox were entirely encased, and the panelling extended forward to form a voluminous front mudguard, wide enough to shroud the wheel from lock to lock.

The sprung saddle was no higher than the top of the wheels, and the rider had an arm-chair posture, with forward-placed inclined footboards and rearswept handlebar grips.

So far as road filth and oil were concerned, the Ner-a-Car could be ridden in a natty suit – or skirt for that matter, for it was a hit with the ladies. But the elements are not so easily catered for, and I wore the heavy garb of the period for my test.

My immediate reaction was disconcerting.

In appropriate garb, the author tries a 1925 Ner-a-Car for stability on a snowy day nearly 30 years after the machine was made

The meagre steering lock (turning circle 19ft 6in), long wheelbase (59in) and above all the geared-up steering combined to make the machine feel very strange compared with the compact Norton twin I had just ridden.

But all sense of strangeness vanished within a few turns of the wheels, to be replaced by a feeling of utter stability. If ever a machine needed its handlebar for little else but mounting the controls, that machine was the Ner-a-Car.

Sitting bolt upright with arms folded, I steered a dead-straight course at speeds down to 12mph – all that was necessary to turn was to press lightly on the inside footboard.

In spite of the conditions, the only limit to banking was the footboards grounding. Indeed, a series of gutter-to-gutter swerves, scraping the boards alternately, detracted not the slightest from the uncanny sense of security. Given 20ft or more of space, I turned tight circles in bottom gear on full lean until I was quite dizzy.

The secret? I concluded it was the ultra-low centre of gravity more than the steering layout, although that, of course, contributed to the low centre of gravity. Unquestionably, the Ner-a-Car must have been well ahead of its contemporaries for stability.

Manufacture began in 1921 at Syracuse, New York. The engine was a 211cc two-stroke single, with both ignition and direct lighting (twin headlamps) supplied from a

flywheel generator. The machine weighed 165lb and cost 225 dollars, the equivalent of £56 in those days, though the British importers (The Inter-Continental Engine Company, in London) marked it up at 66 guineas when they first displayed it, at the 1921 TT.

Then Sheffield-Simplex, car manufacturers at Kingston-on-Thames, were licensed to produce a British version, and they boosted the engine size to 285cc (70×74mm). At first, lighting was by a single electric head-lamp, later changed to an acetylene lamp.

The highly unusual friction drive was retained. In this, a bronze disc on the rear face of the transverse flywheel drove a re-

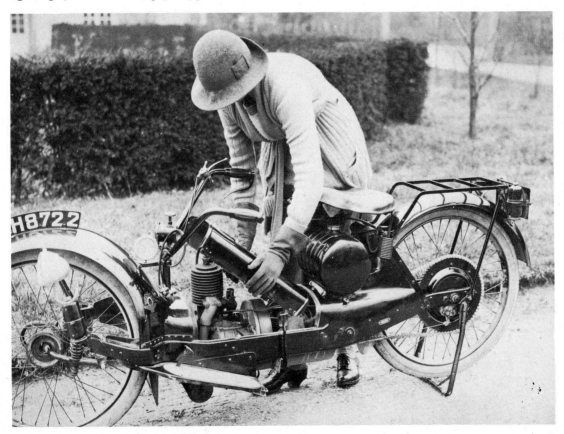

newable fibre ring on a light-alloy wheel splined on the right-hand side of a cross-shaft which had the final-drive chain sprocket fixed on the left-hand end. To lower the friction-drive ratio, the gear lever pushed the aluminium wheel inward across the fly-wheel face against spring pressure. While in theory this could provide a stepless variation, five notches in the lever quadrant gave five distinct ratios, ranging from approximately 10:1 to 5:1.

The clutch was even stranger. Twisting the left handlebar grip pulled the right-hand end of the cross-shaft rearward, so disengaging the drive. Naturally, the pivoted end of the shaft had a self-aligning bearing.

The British licensees soon added more powerful models, with 350cc Blackburne side-valve and overhead-valve engines, and three-speed countershaft gearboxes. Prices plummeted from £57 10s to £39 10s for the two-stroke Model B, £49 10s for the side-valve Model C and £59 10s for the ohv Sports C solo, or £72 with sidecar.

In long-distance road trials, the Ner-a-Car became a byword for reliability, winning gold, silver and bronze medals galore, and two team prizes, including that in the 1925 ACU 1000-mile Stock Machine Trial.

Publicity stunts, too, helped put the Ner-a-Car on the map. Mrs G.M. Jackson completed a 1000-mile ACU-observed test on the two-stroke model without stopping the engine. Despite persistent rain and cold winds, she averaged 190 miles a day with no mechanical bother and very little splash on her clothing. In her one-and-only skid, she had the presence of mind to whip out the clutch and prevent the engine stalling.

About a month later, Mabel Lockwood-Tatham carried out a press test of a similar model. Riding 'no hands' with great confidence, she was surprised to see her escort, on similar models, either standing on the engine casing with hands in pockets, or lying flat on their backs on the saddle. Such gimmicks proved the stability of the Ner-a-Car.

For 1926 Sheffield-Simplex introduced an £85 de-luxe model with quarter-elliptic, pivoted-fork rear springing, air-cushion bucket seat, adjustable Triplex screen and and an instrument panel with a rain scuttle over the rider's knees.

A countershaft behind the gearbox, co-axial with the suspension pivot, kept rear-chain tension constant. And though the springing lengthened the wheelbase to an ungainly 68½in, a road test proclaimed the model as steady as ever.

But, although Sheffield-Simplex advertised earls, duchesses, viscounts and other aristocrats among their customers, the Ner-a-Car foundered on an all-too-familiar rock. It was too unconventional and highly civilised, at a time when after four years of war and austerity the demand for conventional sports machines was stronger than ever.

The Ner-a-Car could no more adapt to the sporting fashion than could the dinosaur to fundamental changes in the environment. And it died – the Ner-a-Car, that is – in the autumn of 1926.

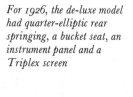

For 1926, the de-luxe model had quarter-elliptic rear springing, a bucket seat, an instrument panel and a Triplex screen

Triumph Ricardo

Harry Ricardo, who was to be knighted for his research, was one of those early fundamentalists who recognised that the heart of an engine is the combustion chamber, with its associated porting. Commissioned to design a 500cc super-sports engine for Triumph in 1921, he plumped for four valves (in parallel pairs at 90 degrees), a central sparking plug and a concave piston crown.

The reasoning behind the double valves was twofold. Since each valve head would be more than half the diameter of a single valve, there would be an overall increase in opening area, hence deeper breathing. Then, the reciprocating mass of each valve would be much lighter, permitting higher revs without valve float, to take better advantage of the freer breathing.

The central plug would cut maximum flame travel by nearly a half, making for more efficient combustion, while the concave crown was a concession to the popular belief that the theoretically ideal combustion-chamber shape, though unattainable practically, was a sphere with the ignition point in the centre.

If much of this (save for the piston crown) smacks of the world-beating Honda racers of the 1960s – and subsequent equally successful racing car engines – that shows how advanced were Ricardo's ideas. Initially, though, the full gains were not realised, because of the use of pushrod valve operation (with its flexure and extra reciprocating parts), splash lubrication (inadequate for sustained high revs) and long-stroke cylinder dimensions (80·5 × 98mm), which restricted valve size.

The phenomenal success of Joe Craig's two-valve works Nortons led European engineers to virtually abandon the four-valve layout in the early 1930s. Some 30 years were to pass before Honda exploited it to the full by using multi cylinders for higher revs,

Except for the cylinder and head, the original Triumph Ricardo was virtually the well-established Model H. The wet sump was replenished from the seat-tube tank by a foot-operated pump

double overhead camshafts for minimum reciprocating weight and precise timing, pressure oiling for high-speed stamina, and oversquare cylinders for larger valves.

Moreover, by Honda's time the crucial importance of port forms and gas resonances was recognised. Their tuned inlet tracts had a long, knife-edge dividing wall, whereas the Triumph induction tract was relatively short, with a blunt wall between the two valves.

To give rapid effective valve opening, the Triumph not only had 30-degree valve seats (instead of the usual 45 degrees). But, for the first time on a motor cycle, the heads of the inlet valves were masked by being slightly recessed in the cylinder head.

This meant that the initial opening and final closing (where the cam form was gentle for quiet operation) were ineffective. But the effective opening and closing, once the valve heads were clear of the pockets, were quite sudden. Incidentally, spring pressure was only 25lb with the valves seated.

To minimise distortion the cylinder, machined from a steel billet, was absolutely symmetrical. The five equally-spaced head-retaining bolts ran right down to the bottom fins to keep their bosses as far as possible from the ground head joint and so avoid warping.

At 14oz, including the two rings and 17mm diameter gudgeon pin, the piston was one of the lightest for a big single – not surprising, since it was in aluminium, of slipper type and with several large holes cut in the thrust faces.

Ricardo's design finished at the cylinder base. From the crankcase mouth down, the engine was based on the well-established 550cc side-valve Model H, as were the cycle parts. The crankcase was flat at the bottom to form a small sump, replenished from time to time from a half-gallon tank behind the seat tube by a foot-operated pump.

Naturally, in view of the smaller engine size, flywheel diameter was slightly reduced, with a consequent lessening in oil drag. Width of the H-section connecting rod was increased but the two-row roller big end was retained.

Transmission was by a $\frac{1}{4} \times \frac{5}{8}$in primary chain, through a clutch embodying a shock absorber, to a two-speed countershaft gearbox with cross-over drive.

After exhaustive bench tests, a fully equipped, street-legal Model R (as it was later catalogued) was taken to Brooklands by George Shemans and put through the torture of a flat-out lap in bottom gear. True, the ratio was not all that low (5·6:1) but Shemans averaged 60mph from a standing

start, revving to about 4600rpm, and finished with the engine remarkably cool.

Before long, more than 100 laps were amassed, average speeds ranging from 65 to 79mph, and more speed was confidently expected, for dynamometer tests showed the engine to be putting out a healthy 20bhp.

As part of a fact-finding exercise – for the engine was still experimental – three Model Rs were entered for the 1921 Senior TT as second string to the side-valve jobs. Shemans, Stan Gill and Chas Sgonina were to have the Ricardo engines.

Early in practising it was found that the engine performance of both models was more than a match for the handling, and Druid front forks were fitted for the race. But, of the Riccies, only Shemans finished. He was a lowly 16th, overshadowed by Jack Watson-Bourne – fifth on the first side-valve machine – and Fred Edmond, who made the fastest lap at 56·4mph, on another side-valve machine, before being slowed by a split oil tank.

Further development paid off handsomely, and, in a publicity exercise at Brooklands just before the London Show, Frank Halford (later to earn fame as an aircraft designer and managing director of De

Above *Walter Brandish at Creg-ny-Baa in the 1922 Senior TT. By finishing second in only his second Isle of Man visit, he amply proved the potential of that year's Ricardo*

Left *a 1924 model. Interesting differences from the original (page 33) include the carburettor and exhaust, the side sparking plug and the front fork and brake*

Opposite *the sparking plug was central and each pair of valves was operated by a rocker with parallel arms*

Havilland) pushed the 500cc hour record up to 76·74 miles, the 50-mile record to 77·27 mph and the flying-start mile to 83·91 mph.

For 1922, the cylinder was an iron casting, with deeper fins, and the dimensions were altered to 85×88mm to permit bigger valves, which increased opening area by 25 per cent. The valve gear was beefed up, the cams widened and the oiling changed to dry sump, with a double-plunger pump. A new front fork, made under Druid patents, was fitted and the gearbox had three speeds.

Tests showed the bike to be much faster. Indeed Walter Brandish, in only his second year in the Island, averaged 56·52mph to finish runner-up to Alec Bennett (Sunbeam) in the Senior TT despite the failure of middle gear at the halfway stage.

The lessons learned in the TT were promptly incorporated in the following year's production Model R, which chalked up early race wins in Belgium, Italy and Ceylon, filled the first three places in the Liège–Paris–Liège marathon and won gold medals in the International Six Days Trial.

Strong favourite to crown the Riccy's reputation by winning the Senior TT, Brandish dominated the practising. But he overstretched his luck when running round a slower rider on the tricky left-hander between Creg-ny-Baa and Hillberry. Clouting the high bank, he broke a leg, and the corner has borne his name ever since.

Regrettably, that put paid to development of the Model R. It remained in the catalogue and retained its popularity for a further four years, but the factory switched development in 1924 to a two-valver on which Victor Horsman had been enhancing his already fine reputation at Brooklands.

Two years later it was incorporated in the range as the Model TT, costing £66 to the Riccy's £55. And in 1927 it carried Tommy Simister into third place in the Senior TT.

The shadow of the great economic depression was darkening the industry, and when Triumph cut their range from eight models to four in 1928, the Riccy was one of the absentees. But the seeds of four-valve thinking had been sown, to blossom with such devastating effect some 40 years later in Japan.

36

Brough Superior vee-twin

Quality, not quantity, was the hallmark of the Brough Superior. For some 20-odd years before the Second World War, the specifications were so lavish, the finish so superlative and the prices so high, that the marque was known far and wide as the Rolls-Royce of motor cycles. Yet the Nottingham factory's total output in all that time was fewer than 3000 machines. Some models had a run of a mere nine or ten, and at least three of the most exotic projects – a transverse vee-four, ditto vee-twin and a Swiss-engined four-in-line – were strictly one-offs.

The most renowned of all the Brough Superiors, however, were the husky big twins – mostly of 1000cc, but as small as 500cc and as large as 1150cc. By far the most exciting model technically, the flat-four Dream, embodied so much novelty as to warrant a later chapter to itself.

George Brough was as much a publicist as a perfectionist. Scarcely a London Show went by but what he stole the limelight with some new and sensational design. Among his customers was the legendary Lawrence of Arabia, who waxed lyrical in print over the joys of his succession of big twins.

Not only George himself, but some of the most eminent speedmen of their day – including Bert Le Vack, Ted Baragwanath, Freddie Dixon, Eric Fernihough and Noel Pope – earned the marque undying fame on the sprint strips and beaches, at Brooklands and in the world-record lists.

Though it is commonly done, strictly it is wrong to refer to Brough Superiors simply as Broughs. That was a separate make, produced by George's father, William, in another part of Nottingham. The first machine, in 1902, was a pedal-assisted single, after which there were vee-twins and flat twins up to 1926. George left the business in 1919 to set up on his own, and shrewdly tacked the word Superior on to the name.

His first model was typical of what was to form the bulk of his output. Aimed at the connoisseur, it had a 1000cc ($90 \times 77.5\text{mm} \times 2$), overhead-valve, 50-degree vee-twin JAP engine. But, unlike the JAPs supplied to other makers, it had the overhead-valve gear

George Brough on 'Old Bill', the 1923 40-bhp SS80 on which he won innumerable sprints and turned the first Brooklands 100-mph lap by a side-valve machine

1936 version of the famous overhead-valve SS100, with Castle bottom-link front fork and AMC engine with hairpin valve springs

SS100, with an improved engine, cradle frame, Castle bottom-link front fork and a guarantee of 100mph. A year later it was marketed with full road equipment as the Alpine Grand Sports, and in pure racing trim as the Pendine.

Over the years, both the SS80 and SS100 were developed, with the adoption of Matchless engines and rear springing, first of pivoted-fork type, then plunger. But, for the less affluent, George Brough offered a 680cc ohv twin, a seven-fifty side-valve and even a five-hundred, with an engine based on JAP's 1930 TT twin. Interspersed among all these twins were the 1000cc vee-four (in 1927), with the cylinder banks at 60 degrees, and the 900cc straight four a year later – both, surprisingly, with chain drive, despite the crankshaft lying fore and aft.

Even more radical was the 800cc straight four introduced in 1931. This model had not only the refinement of shaft drive, but twin rear wheels, with the shaft and bevels between them, and the brake drum in the right-hand hub. The engine was an enlarged version of that fitted to the Austin Seven car, with water cooling and electric starting. Even the reverse gear was retained.

For sidecar duty, the size of the side-valve engine was pushed up to 1100cc in 1933, and an ingenious, foot-controlled banking sidecar was designed to suit shortly afterwards.

Then, for 1938, came the one-off transverse vee-twin, with an SS80 Matchless side-valve engine coupled to an Austin four-speed synchromesh gearbox. Since the clutch had both hand and foot controls on the left, the gear and brake pedals were together on the right. Final drive was again by chain.

But, if the most widely known Brough Superiors were the 1000cc ohv twins, then the most revered of those were the racing versions ridden by Eric Fernihough, Ted Baragwanath and Noel Pope – and even that selection does scant justice to many another intrepid speedman, such as one-time world-record holders Bert Le Vack, Freddie Dixon and Alan Bruce.

Tall, bespectacled and a Master of Arts, Fernihough was a patriot to his fingertips, and brave with it. Switching from Excelsior tiddlers to the thundering big twins with contemptuous ease, he fought a bitter battle on a shoestring against Ernst Henne and the organised might of BMW for the world speed record.

With neither dynamometer nor wind-tunnel facilities, he did his tuning and streamlining on a suck-it-and-see basis. Yet, in 1935, he lifted the Brooklands lap record

and the lower ends of the cylinders plated, while the crankcase was sandblasted.

Bulbous at the front, wedge-shaped at the rear, the black-and-silver tank was stylish in the inimitable BS way, and it was also lined in pure gold leaf. The frame was claimed to have four coats of best black enamel on a rubber-solution base for rust prevention.

Within about three years, there was also a choice of a side-valve JAP engine, Swiss MAGs of 750 and 1000cc, with overhead inlet and side exhaust valves, and a sweet and silent Barr and Stroud sleeve-valve engine – all vee-twins.

In 1923 the famous SS80 1000cc side-valve was born and George himself really put it on the sporting map. On his personal model – first nicknamed Spit and Polish, then Old Bill – he not only won 51 of his 52 sprints but also turned the first-ever 100-mph lap of Brooklands' concrete bowl with a side-valve machine.

Then, for the Olympia Show of 1924, the original ohv twin was redesigned as the

to 123·58mph without benefit of super-charging, to gain his Double Gold Star for a lap at more than two miles a minute. Then, with the engine blown, he set his sights on the world record, making the 1000-mile trip to Gyon, in Hungary, for want of a suitable stretch nearer home. There, in 1936, he raised the flying-mile record to 163·82mph but failed to wrest the faster kilometre record from Henne. A year later, he took the solo record at 169·79mph and the sidecar at 137·11mph, though a virtual novice on three wheels!

The Gyon road was narrow, bumpy and exposed to strong, changeable winds. And in the spring of 1938, tilting at Henne's 173·67 mph, Ferni met his untimely end. At an estimated 180mph, the wind reacted on the partial streamlining and either blew or lifted the bike off course. For some 200 yards Ferni grappled with his projectile in the shallow ditch flanking the road. Then came the final prang – and Ferni's superhuman endeavours were posthumously commemorated in a plaque on the BMCRC clubhouse wall at Brooklands in 1939.

Baragwanath's long and illustrious career with a Brough Superior outfit, both unblown and blown, was a saga of enterprise, endea-vour and achievement. From his very first season on it (1927) he achieved the highest honours – world standing-start records, countless sprint and track wins, a Brooklands sidecar Gold Star and lap record.

Incongruously addicted to wearing a wing

collar under his leathers, he was one of the most spectacular performers on the banked concrete oval. With neither rev counter nor boost gauge to guide him, he played it by ear. With indomitable courage and strength, he dwarfed his rivals at Brooklands until he retired at the age of 50, after turning upward of 200 laps in excess of 100mph.

Above *on the supercharged version of his 1000cc Brough Superior, Fernihough is pushed off at Brooklands.* Below *the most successful sidecar outfit ever at Brooklands. Baragwanath poses on the machine on which he did more than 200 ton laps*

39

Right *Noel Pope, ultimate solo and sidecar record holder at Brooklands, on the ex-Baragwanath machine he prepared for a world-record bid in 1949*

Below *for his ill-fated outing on the Bonneville Salt Flats, Pope fitted his Brough Superior with this aluminium shell, calculated to boost top speed to 209mph*

It was entirely fitting that a machine with so glorious a record should then be acquired by a man whose subsequent exploits on it were nothing short of heroic – Noel Pope. Unhitching the sidecar, he straight away upped the Brooklands solo lap record to 120.59mph in 1935, so earning the first-ever Double Gold Star.

After an interlude racing mostly abroad, he refocussed his attentions on Brooklands, gaining his sidecar Gold Star and the final lap record at 106·6mph, before electrifying the onlookers with a meteoric solo lap record of 124·5mph just before the war.

Some 10 years later, in 1949, Pope completely enclosed the bike in a streamline shell calculated to boost its speed to 209mph, and set sail for Utah with the intention of annihilating the world record.

But the aerodynamics, like Ferni's, were less than perfect, and Pope's bid ended in a spectacular prang at about 150mph, from which he fortunately walked away. Streamline shells have since become essential for world-record speeds, but the name of Brough Superior is just a memory.

Ariel Square Four

Nowadays, four-cylinder roadsters are commonplace, and they all have the run-of-the-mill cylinder arrangement – in line across the frame. But in the 1930s, 1940s and 1950s, the ownership of a four set you apart as a member of a tiny élite, and, unless your bike was a Brough Superior, the cylinder arrangement was unique. For, as its name implied, the Ariel Square Four – made altogether in three sizes and various guises – had each cylinder at the corner of a square, with two 180-degree crankshafts coupled together.

The very mention of coupled crankshafts brings frowns to the faces of production engineers. The gears, they say, are costly, and they rattle, especially when the crankcase warms up and the consequent expansion moves the crankshaft axes farther apart.

But Edward Turner, who dreamed up the square four layout late in 1928, was shrewd enough to recognise that all engineering design is a compromise. Set the cylinders across the frame, he thought, and you have ungainly width, especially if the primary drive is taken from one end of the crankshaft. Set them in line astern and you have an unwieldy wheelbase as well as cooling prob-lems, particularly for the third cylinder.

Flat fours and vee-fours also have their problems – cylinder-head vulnerability in the first case, and the commitment to shaft drive in both cases, unless you use expensive bevel gears to turn the crankshaft motion through 90 degrees for final chain drive.

The compact square-four layout offered reasonably narrow width, a standard wheel-base, conventional chain drive and no cooling difficulties; the problem of gear rattle with crankcase expansion could be alleviated by a special tooth form.

Ariel took up Turner's layout enthusiasti-cally. With diagonally-opposed pistons mov-ing in step, all primary inertia forces were cancelled out, while the much smaller secondaries – acting upward at top and bottom dead centres, downward at mid-stroke – were no worse than in a conventional car engine. So there was every prospect, not only of outstanding mechanical balance, but also of ultra-smooth torque from lots of tiny power impulses instead of widely-spaced thumps.

Development of Britain's first four took time. So light was the original prototype engine that it slotted handily into the frame

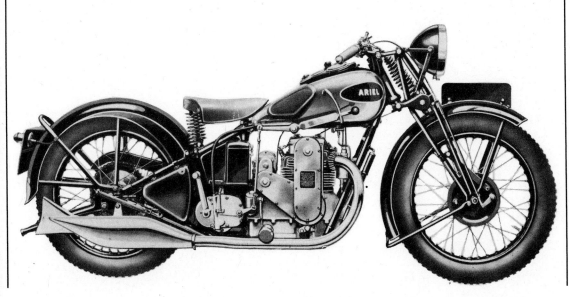

First of a long line of Square Fours, the 1931 four-speed 500cc (51 × 61mm) model had a chain-driven overhead camshaft, and the carburettor at the front of the cylinder head

of the standard 250cc single, while the overall width was narrowed by building the three-speed gearbox integrally with the crankcase and taking the primary drive from the coupling gear in the middle of the rear crankshaft.

The bike delighted the testers. It could be started by sitting side-saddle and pushing off with one leg. But skimpy cylinder-head finning and inadequate airflow under the overhead cambox led to overheating and consequent loss of power on sustained full throttle. Anyway it was felt that the layout embodied too many novelties for commercial success.

Subsequent prototypes put on weight and veered towards conformity. Even so, when the first production Square Four was unveiled at Olympia in the autumn of 1930, it took the Show by storm.

Installed in the duplex frame of the similar capacity single, the 500cc (51 × 61 mm) engine had a chain-driven overhead camshaft, while the induction tract from the forward-mounted Amal carburettor led to the middle of a cross-shape port layout. The straight-tooth coupling gears in the middle of the crankshafts were enclosed in a separate chamber. Three of the four cranks were overhung to permit the use of roller big-end bearings. The left-side rear crank, however, had a conventional outer web and mainshaft, to carry the chain sprocket for the

drive to the four-speed Burman gearbox.

Car-fashion, the crankcase was split horizontally, with the oil sump in the bottom half, although the main bearings were supported from the top. Driven from the middle of the front crankshaft was a half-time shaft carrying two sprockets, one for the camshaft drive, the other for the Lucas Magdyno.

Although it had been conceived as a luxury solo, the Square Four made an immediate appeal to sidecar men. So the bore size was increased to 56mm to give 600cc, and the smaller model was soon dropped. Yet it was in solo trim, and supercharged at that, that the early ohc version achieved its greatest fame.

Ben Bickell, one of the stars of the Brooklands outer circuit, reckoned it was just the job for his bid for the *Motor Cycle* cup – offered for the first British 500cc multi to put 100 miles in an hour. Acquiring a large-mileage demonstration six-hundred in 1933, he brought it within the 500cc limit by fitting a 51mm-bore cylinder block. The seat tube was then hacked out of the frame and replaced by a pair of $\frac{1}{4}$in-thick steel plates, housing a Powerplus blower, chain driven from an extra sprocket on the clutch drum.

Sandwiched between the three-speed Burman gearbox and the rear wheel, the carburettor fed the blower at the bottom, while the induction pipe from the top swept round the left side of the cylinder block to the inlet port. Right from the start, 100-mph laps were commonplace. Indeed, in 1934, Bickell got the Ariel round at 111·42mph. But his every attempt at the hour was foiled by failure of the cylinder-head gasket.

As the six-hundred continued in production year by year, two demands became ever more insistent. One was for more flywheel inertia, the other for greater engine capacity.

By restricting the diameter of the flywheel discs, the central coupling gears put a limit on the flywheel inertia. So the overhung-crank layout was abandoned in favour of full crankshafts (with split big-end bearings) and the coupling gears were moved into a compartment on the left side of the crankcase.

Since each crankshaft incorporated a central flange, it was only necessary to bolt the front and rear flywheels to opposite sides of the flanges for the wheels to overlap, so that they could be made considerably larger.

At the same time, the stroke was increased to 75mm, so that a cylinder block with 50·4 mm bores gave 600cc, while the block with 65mm bores gave 1000cc. Other main changes were to pushrod valve operation, a vertically-split crankcase, dry-sump oiling (with a separate six-pint tank) and a rear-mounted Solex carburettor.

Only the 1000cc version survived the war. It acquired a telescopic front fork and optional rear springing, and it clearly be-

came much too heavy. So, for 1949, the weight was slashed by no less than ½cwt by rehashing the engine with an aluminium cylinder block and head and coil ignition. The quicker heat dissipation from the engine enhanced its stamina, too.

Above *Motor Cycling road-tester Charlie Markham samples a 1948 1000cc (65 × 75mm) 4G with telescopic front fork*

Below *to cut weight drastically in 1949, both cylinder block and head were changed from iron to aluminium alloy. Note the link-type rear springing*

It was that improvement in cooling that made possible the most exciting Square Four of them all – the four-pipe Mark II, with higher compression and gearing, a five-gallon tank, gear-type oil pumps, and power boosted to 42bhp at 5800rpm – a veritable Jekyll-and-Hyde machine that could be docile or ferocious at a flick of the wrist.

On the *Motor Cycle* test model I logged close on 2000 miles in a couple of enthralling weekends, wearing the rear tyre smooth in the process. With neither the help of motorways nor the hindrance of a 70mph limit, I headed from London to Troon early in 1953 to indulge in some private airfield racing with the up-and-coming Bob McIntyre.

In the teeth of a near-gale, the Mark II comfortably put 158 miles into the first 2¼

hours (a 70mph average) before the ammeter succumbed to the secondary vibrations. After a repair, the weather did its worst, with the sheer purgatory of lashing rain and gales, especially from Scotch Corner to Penrith. Yet the Ariel's time for the 406 miles was seven hours dead, an average of 58mph, with neither bike nor rider feeling the strain at the end.

What if my deliberate attempt to burst the engine on the return run from a MIRA test session had the aristocratic Ariel weaving and pitching down the bumpy A5 like a 100-mph corkscrew? And what if the sustained full bore ride caught me out, with two gallons of petrol slopping through the jets in a mere 70 miles? You can't have it all ways, can you?

The most exciting of all Square Four engines, the four-pipe Mark II, introduced in 1953 with higher compression and gear-pump oiling. Power was 42 bhp at 5800rpm

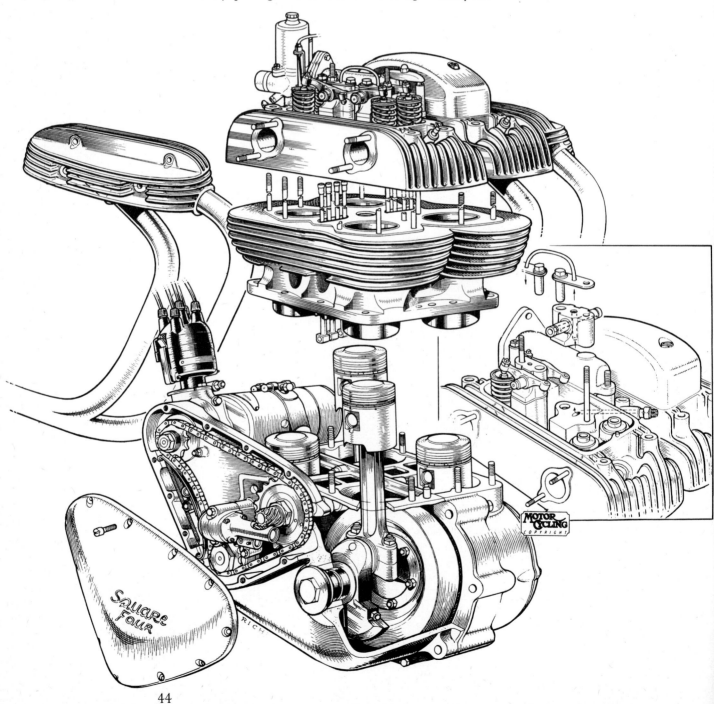

Overhead Camshaft Norton

Unforgettable. Applied to the glorious history of the overhead-camshaft racing Norton, that word is no exaggeration. One of the most stark and functional machines ever to induce sheer despair in the hearts of the opposition, it made its début in a blaze of glory with Alec Bennett's Senior TT win in the Isle of Man in 1927, and died extraordinarily hard nearly 30 years later.

During all that time, and longer, the makers' advertising slogan was 'Unapproachable'. Eventually the march of progress overtook that proud boast when the Italian fours made a dodo of the big single. But the memory of Norton's long heyday does not fade.

Although the highest respect is due both to the original designer, Walter Moore (later to produce a similar machine for NSU), and to Arthur Carroll, who redesigned the engine a few years later, the Norton legend stands chiefly as a monument to that most single-minded and painstaking of development engineers, Joe Craig. Both before and after the war, his works bikes acted like a magnet to a galaxy of superstars, including Stanley Woods, Tim Hunt, Jimmy Simpson, Jimmy Guthrie, Freddie Frith, Harold Daniell, Geoff Duke, Artie Bell, Reg Armstrong, Ray Amm and sidecar driver Eric Oliver.

Thirty international TT wins fell to it, countless other grands prix, eight individual and eight manufacturers' world championships and a few world one-hour records – the most spectacular being Amm's 133·5 miles on a streamlined 'kneeler' in 1953.

From 1931 until the outbreak of war, the 500cc and 350cc black-and-silver singles

Alec Bennett, who first put the 500cc overhead-camshaft Norton single on the map by winning the 1927 Senior TT

practically monopolised the TT, toughest of all the grands prix, being beaten in only two Seniors (by multis) and two Juniors (by Velocettes). The war set the multis back for a time, for they owed their initial superiority chiefly to supercharging, which was subsequently banned. And so the pre-war Nortons dominated the first three post-war Seniors, too.

Then in the early 1950s, came a repetition of Norton's near-invincibility of the 1930s. With intense engine development, a fresh breed of stars and a new frame that gave them so vast an improvement in control and comfort as to be nicknamed the featherbed, the works team extended the competitiveness of the big racing single practically to the limit.

Sire of that long line of classic-race winners, Walter Moore's original overhead-camshaft five-hundred was ridden in the 1927 TT by Woods (who broke the lap record) and Craig, as well as by Bennett, the winner. It had a long-stroke (79 × 100mm) engine – with iron cylinder and head, single camshaft and internal flywheels – three speeds, a solid frame, a friction-damped girder front fork and single-leading-shoe brakes. A year later it was partnered by a basically similar three-fifty with cylinder dimensions of 71 × 88mm.

Step by step, Joe Craig's evolutionary work led to short-stroke dimensions – 90 × 78·4mm for the bigger engine, 78 × 73mm for the smaller – light-alloy cylinder and head, twin camshafts, outside flywheel, four

speeds, rear springing (first plunger type, then pivoted fork), telescopic front springing and two leading shoes in the front brake. And along the way the bigger engine became the first of its size to develop 50bhp.

That's the bare bones of it. The full details would fill a book, so let's select some of the more interesting.

In Walter Moore's design, the cams were separate for individual timing. The rocker arms were separate from the shafts, too, the outer arms being a taper fit, the inner ones having hardened heels to bear on the cams. In the camshaft drive, the lower vertical bevel gear was threaded at the top for clamping into the inner race of its ball bearing. And the vertical shaft was splined into its bevels at both ends.

To spread the load as evenly as possible over the teeth, the 2:1 reduction was shared between the upper and lower pairs of bevels – the so-called hunting-tooth principle.

Worm driven, the double rotary-plunger oil pump had a separate feed to the ohc mechanism, with drainage through the shaft tube. When, in spite of the cylinder and head being cast in iron, the engine was found to run extremely cool (on a 50/50 petrol-benzole mixture of about 80 octane), the compression ratio was raised from 6·4:1 to 7:1.

Though the Sturmey Archer gearbox was controlled by foot, there was no positive-stop mechanism, the pedal having three different positions. A cradle frame was designed to supersede the diamond frame used with the earlier pushrod engine.

When rehashing the engines for 1930, Arthur Carroll collaborated with Joe Craig, who was already in charge of development. The impact was soon felt, not only in Norton's near-monopoly of the 1931 Senior and Junior TTs, but also in Bill Lacey's 110·8-mile one-hour record at Montlhéry, near Paris, three months later.

For 1932, snubber springs superseded friction damping for the front forks, and the cylinder heads were cast in aluminium-bronze. The following year there were bi-metal heads and barrels and, in 1934, hair-pin valve springs, exhaust megaphones and dual ignition. And although Norton pride was dented when Stanley Woods (Moto Guzzi) beat Jimmy Guthrie by four seconds in the 1935 Senior TT, there was compensation when Guthrie later raised the hour hour record to 114·09mph at Montlhéry.

Double camshafts were tried in 1936, but not raced until the following year. At about that time, too, a series of stroke shortenings began, with the intention of per-

In the first ohc Norton engine (79 × 100mm), the vertical shaft was splined into the upper and lower bevel gears. The rocker arms were separate from their shafts. Oil fed to the cambox drained down the vertical-shaft tube

Shots from Norton's pre-war era. Left a typical refuelling shot from the 1930 Senior TT. Above development chief Joe Craig (on rider's left) looks as happy as Tim Hunt, who has just won the 1931 Junior TT. Top left Jimmie Guthrie is jarred off the seat during his heroic 114·09-mile hour record at Montlhéry in 1935

Pre-war Norton star
Harold Daniell roars past
Kate's Cottage on his 91-mph
record lap in winning his
first TT – the 1938 Senior

Post-war Norton star Geoff
Duke aviates his featherbed
works three-fifty in winning
the 1952 Junior TT

mitting bigger valves and higher peak rpm.

In speeding to overhaul Stanley Woods (Velocette), following Guthrie's fifth-lap retirement in the 1937 Senior TT, Freddie Frith turned the first 90-mph lap in the Isle of Man.

Telescopic front springing, cone hubs and brake ventilation came in 1938, as did Harold Daniell's 91-mph TT lap – a record that was to stand for 12 years, unbeaten even by the supercharged BMWs of Georg Meier and Jock West that headed Frith's Norton in the 1939 Senior.

After the war, development restarted quietly enough with a twin-leading-shoe front brake in 1948, along with steady engine development. But the flood was unleashed by the coincidence of the featherbed frame with the sheer genius of Geoff Duke's riding. While his incomparable skills more than offset the extra power and speed of the Italian fours, Craig squeezed more performance and consistency out of the Nortons with extended cylinder finning, rotating-magnet magnetos, oil cooling of the exhaust-

48

T.D.COLLINS

valve guides, and weir-type carburettors.

In the final analysis, the works Nortons of both sizes had 9in diameter external flywheels, to maintain the necessary flywheel inertia, while both piston stroke and connecting-rod length were shortened to reduce engine height. The crankshaft was a two-piece forging in KE805 steel, with integral mainshafts, webs and bobweights, and the hollow crankpin formed with the drive-side half, which incorporated a rubber transmission shock absorber.

The Al-Fin barrels were almost swallowed by the crankcase mouth, leaving room for only six-cylinder fins on the three-fifty, eight on the five-hundred. Included angle of the valves was a comparatively narrow 64 degrees, and the combustion chambers were further compacted by squish bands on both sides.

Compression ratios were 10·8:1 (350cc) and 10·4:1 (500cc), carburettor sizes $1\frac{3}{16}$ in and $1\frac{13}{32}$ in respectively, with a downdraught angle of 20 degrees.

Oil of SAE20 viscosity was fed to the big end and cambox at the rate of 30 gallons an hour at 6000rpm, and scavenged from both the crankcase and the lower bevel housing. Its running temperature was a modest 60 degrees C.

After Norton officially withdrew from racing at the end of 1954, Moto Guzzi kept the single-cylinder flag flying for a further three years. Indeed, a suspiciously similar Norton, with horizontal cylinder and integral gearbox had been scheduled for 1955.

But, under the fixed-capacity formula, the big single – British or Italian – was inevitably forced to bow to the power superiority of the multi.

Sectioned drawing of one of the last catalogued Manx Norton five-hundreds. Slung low in the duplex-loop frame, the engine had two pairs of bevels and five spur gears in the camshaft drive. Double leading shoes were used in the front brake

Overhead Camshaft Velocette

A sure sign of sound design is staying power. When, in 1925, Velocette took the bold step of switching straight from small two-strokes to a high-performance overhead-camshaft three-fifty, that Model K incorporated several unusual design features. These were not only justified by almost instant success; they also stayed basically unchanged until production of that most famous of all ohc Velocettes, the KTT racer, ceased in the early 1950s.

Among the unusual features was an inboard primary drive, which left the gearbox final-drive sprocket very accessible for the simplest possible change of overall ratios in racing. More important, it enabled the crankcase to be kept very narrow, with the single main bearings closely spaced and in direct line with the walls of the crankcase and cylinder for really rigid support. Furthermore, since the engine sprocket was hard up against the drive-side bearing, shaft flexure under load was cut to a minimum.

The inboard position of the clutch necessitated a withdrawal system differing from the usual pushrod through the mainshaft. Velos used a self-centring, caged-ball thrust bearing and three hardened pins. Although it has been maligned by riders who didn't take the trouble to master the adjustment drill, when properly set up and adjusted,

this type of clutch was as good as any.

Other details which remained unchanged from first to last were the bore and stroke (74×81 mm), the chain drive to the rear-mounted magneto, the camshaft drive by two pairs of bevel gears (connected by a vertical shaft and two Oldham couplings) and water deflectors on the brake plates.

Incredibly for so new a design (the work of Percy Goodman), the Velo won the 1926 Junior TT when Alec Bennett, shattering lap and race records, trounced the meteoric Jimmy Simpson (AJS) by nearly $10\frac{1}{2}$ minutes in spite of coming a 50-mph cropper at the Nook, within a mile of the finish. It was the very first ohc win in any class of the TT.

Soon Goodman's engineering team was joined by Harold Willis, a first-class rider as well as a superb development engineer – and a fertile inventor of slang. To him the exhaust pipe was a long hole, the plug a candle, the piston a cork; valves were nails, cams were knockers; light alloy was trouble metal, and the bulbous five-gallon tank on the first works five-hundred (in 1934) an ale barrel. But besides such colloquialisms, the race-shop team pioneered a flood of novelties, both basic and detail, that kept them well to the fore in progress and success alike, right up to the war.

The original ohc design was shown at

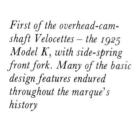

First of the overhead-camshaft Velocettes – the 1925 Model K, with side-spring front fork. Many of the basic design features endured throughout the marque's history

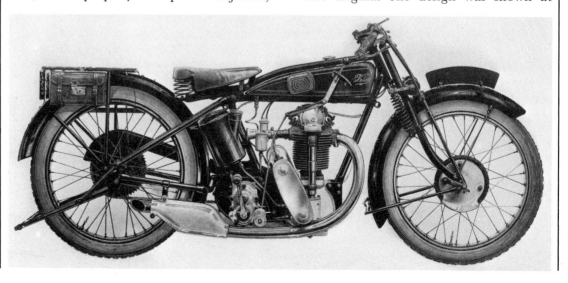

Left *the KN with girder front fork. Velocettes were unusual in having the primary drive inboard of the final drive*

Below *in the year when Velocette pioneered positive-stop foot change (1928), Alec Bennett rounds Governor's Bridge on his way to his second Junior TT win in three years*

Olympia in the autumn of 1924, and some notable alterations were made before it went into production in time for the 1925 Junior TT. The main change concerned the oiling system. Originally the oil gravitated from the tank to a pump on the left-hand end of the camshaft. This kept the cambox filled to a predetermined level, lubricating the rockers, while crankcase depression sucked the overflow down the vertical-shaft tube and into the big end.

For the TT, the pump was shifted into the bottom bevel housing, forcing oil to the big end and up the shaft tube to the cambox. A scavenge pump kept the sump dry. Another change was from roller cam followers, which tended to seize at high revs, to ground skids on the rocker ends. Even so, both the Velos that started in the 1925 TT retired.

For the following year cam and piston mods boosted engine power above 20bhp, while an increase from one plate to three in

51

the clutch coped with the extra urge. Not only did this give Bennett his decisive edge in performance, but the makers cashed in by marketing a super-sports roadster version, the KSS, with a guarantee of 80mph.

To allow a faster oil-circulation rate, the cambox too was scavenged for 1927, by a plunger pump on the end. That year Willis was runner-up in the Junior TT, splitting Freddie Dixon (HRD), the winner, and Simpson (AJS).

A boom year for Velocette followed. Their pioneering of positive-stop foot change (which spread like wildfire throughout the industry) gave their riders such an advantage that Bennett and Willis outclassed the opposition in the Junior TT, the winner (Bennett) turning the first 70-mph lap on a three-fifty. During practice Draper rear springing, with a triangulated and pivoted rear fork (the flying bedstead, according to Willis), was tried but abandoned.

Then, with the compression ratio raised from 7·25:1 to 10·5:1 for alcohol fuel, a TT model was the first three-fifty to cram 100 miles into an hour, adding no less than 7·18

miles to the record. There followed a string of foreign grand prix wins, a host of Brooklands successes and, at Montlhéry, a bag of long-distance world records up to 12 hours.

Once again the manufacturers cashed in by marketing the KTT for £80 in 1929 – the first out-and-out racer ever catalogued. It proved immensely popular and successful. Following Freddie Hicks' record-breaking win in the Junior TT, private KTTs filled the first eight places in the Junior Manx GP and won many a Brooklands Gold Star (on alcohol) for lapping at 100mph.

Hairpin valve springs were introduced in 1932, along with a 14mm plug and down-draught induction. The cambox scavenge pump was changed from plunger type to gears, and the transmission from three speeds to four, with the positive-stop mechanism switched from outside to inside the box. Later, the internal ratchet system was standardised and the earlier design sold to the Scott company.

Another abortive experiment was a long-stroke engine (68 × 96mm) aimed at a more compact combustion chamber.

Engine of the Mark I KTT, the first out-and-out racer ever marketed. It was based on the phenomenally successful works machines

Next significant development on the KTT was a change from iron to aluminium-bronze for the cylinder head on the later Mk IV models. But that is taking us beyond one of Willis' most enterprising experiments – supercharging – which is particularly tricky on a four-stroke single.

Whiffling Clara, as he nicknamed the first blown KTT in 1931, had a Foxwell supercharger with a six-blade eccentric rotor. Since the blower delivered a steady pressure, while the engine breathed in intermittent gasps every two revolutions, a large gas reservoir was installed, pannier fashion, in the right-hand rear triangle of the frame to damp out the pulsations. The basic flaw was that the supercharger blew through the carburettor instead of sucking through it. And that necessitated pressurisation of both tank and float chamber if petrol was to continue to flow to the carburettor and the necessary depression was to be maintained over the jet.

Although it was tried in TT practice, the machine was not raced. For 1932 the simpler arrangement of the blower sucking through the carb and feeding the gas reservoir was adopted, with the throttle control between the reservoir and the inlet valve.

Combining docility with tremendous acceleration, Whiffling Clara nevertheless retired with a broken rocker ('camshaft weevil') in the Junior and a loose jet in the Senior. And that was the end of Velocette's efforts to supercharge a single.

Next came a light-alloy head and full rocker enclosure, with the exposed valves actuated by short tappets; also revised lubrication, with jets squirting oil to the vital parts. The new five-hundred was virtually an 81×96mm version of the three-fifty and weighed only a few pounds more. And both machines continued to be more than a match for anything but Joe Craig's works Nortons.

In 1936 there was both an ill-starred venture into twin camshafts and a highly-successful switch to pivoted-fork rear springing. But that brings us to the era of the unsprung Mk VII KTT and the rear-sprung Mk VIII (page 101) both with massively-finned light-alloy engines – an era that deserves a story of its own.

The simpler (1932) version of 'Whiffling Clara'. Unlike the previous year's blown model, the super-charger sucked through the carburettor and pressurised the triangular gas reservoir above the silencer

Four-valve Rudge

Four decades before Honda revived the idea for classic racing and made a monkey of the opposition, Rudge Whitworth were sold on four-valve cylinder heads. Though the era of five-figure rpm rates in racing was then undreamed-of, doubling up the inlet and exhaust valves made sense to the Coventry engineers – and for much the same reasons as it makes sense today.

For a given cylinder-bore size, they argued, four small valves gave a larger total opening area than two big ones, hence better breathing. And because of the higher ratio of seat area to head size, small exhaust valves ran cooler than large ones.

In the event of over-revving, valve float could be avoided with comparatively light springs. Also, since valve breakage was as pressing a problem as valve float in those days, the relatively greater strength of the smaller valves enhanced reliability.

Finally, the layout was tailor-made for a central sparking plug, giving a much shorter flame travel (though in the earliest four-valve Rudges side plugs were retained).

Two distinct types of four-valve Rudge, both designed by development engineer and race chief George Hack, made an indelible imprint on motor-cycle history. First was the 500cc (85 × 88mm) supersports Ulster model, so named to commemorate Graham Walker's brilliant victory in the 1928 Ulster Grand Prix, the first road race to be won at over 80mph. The valves were in parallel pairs in a pent-roof head, in which a central plug and splayed, not parallel, exhaust ports had not long been adopted.

The other engine type had the valves radially disposed in a part-spherical head and operated by an ingenious system of six roller-bearing rockers. It made a phenomenal, record-splintering one–two–three début in the 1930 Junior TT, won by Tyrell Smith, and then dominated the Lightweight (250cc) TT, where Graham Walker won the following year, and Jimmy Simpson headed another one–two–three in 1934.

Eventually, after one year when it was catalogued with fully radial valves (1932), a patented semi-radial layout was adopted for the Ulster with parallel inlets in a flat head surface, and radial exhausts in a part-spherical portion.

Convinced of the value of road racing in

Straight from the drawing board, the Radial Rudge scooped the first three places in the 1930 Junior TT. Here is the winner, Tyrell Smith, at Quarter Bridge

forcing the pace of development, the factory, under the enthusiastic John Pugh, usually adapted its successful innovations to the following year's production models. Further examples of independence in Rudge thinking were the change to four speeds, long before their rivals, and the use of progressively-coupled 8in-diameter brakes.

In this system the right-side pedal operated the front brake direct by cable, whereas in the rod from the pedal to the rear brake there was an enclosed coil spring to limit pressure and so prevent wheel locking. The front brake had an auxiliary handlebar control. And when foot change was introduced the gear pedal was, at first, on the left.

Had Graham Walker's engine not failed through oil starvation high on Snaefell in the last lap of the 1928 Senior TT, the Rudge Ulster might well have been given another name. For at the start of that lap the burly Walker had an enormous lead of 2½ minutes over the diminutive Charlie Dodson, who gratefully took over to win on his Sunbeam.

Their resumed battle in the Ulster GP two months later was a sizzler. Almost from the start they passed and repassed, the effects of tactics and performance impossible to distinguish. Bar to bar, they thundered into the last lap, and it was only in the closing stages that Walker pulled out an 11-second advantage, his race average of 80·08mph adding some 6mph to the previous record.

There could scarcely have been a more fitting victory on which to base the name of the 85-mph supersports roadster. And, to hammer home the message, Ernie Nott wound up the 1928 season by pushing the world two-hour record up to 100·23mph, including stops for refuelling.

The possibility of lean oil settings was eliminated on the 1929 works racers by changing from total-loss to dry-sump lubrication. Graham Walker again won the Ulster GP at record speed (80·63mph). Nott claimed the world hour record with 106·49 miles, and shared the saddle with Tyrell Smith to lift the two-hour average to 102·87 mph.

When the stylish Walter Handley cakewalked the 1930 Senior TT at record speed in teeming rain, there seemed to be no stopping the pent-roof four-valve Rudge. But even that heroic performance was overshadowed by the masterly showing of the new radial-valvers in the Junior race earlier in the week.

Except for the inevitable bench testing and a brief gallop up the road by Tyrell

Left *from the two pushrod-operated rockers, transverse rockers actuated the radial valves in the Rudge layout*

Below *in 1931 radial valves were adopted on the works two-fifties. Here is Graham Walker after winning the Lightweight TT*

Smith, it was virtually a case of straight from the drawing board to the winners' rostrum. However long the TT survives, no fresh design can hope to eclipse that achievement.

Statistically, it was the first Junior victory at more than 70mph, the last by a pushrod engine. But the real interest lay in the design of the valve gear. The first two rockers, operated by the pushrods, did not open the right-hand valves direct. Instead, they depressed the right-hand ends of two transverse rockers that opened the valves. The left-hand ends of those transverse rockers lifted, with a pure rolling contact, the inner ends of another pair of transverse rockers that opened the left-hand valves.

Not only did this arrangement give a part-spherical combustion chamber, it also allowed slightly more metal between the exhaust-valve seats, and hence reduced the risk of cracking. But the new engines were

Above *the Rudge Ulster of 1933 had radial exhaust valves and parallel inlets.*

Far right *Graham Walker heels through Ramsey in the 1931 Lightweight TT.*

Right *a sectioned drawing of the Ulster engine in its 1937 form, with the valves enclosed*

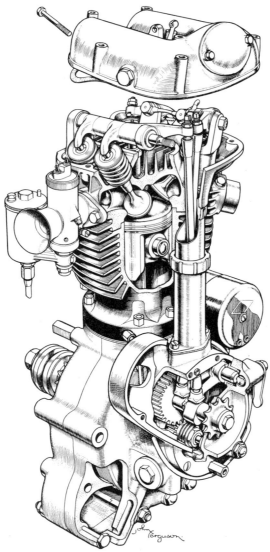

not entirely free from cracks. They developed them at the gudgeon-pin bosses during practice. And new pistons fitted for the race only just lasted out!

When Rudge entered a team of two-fifties of similar design in the following year's Lightweight TT, they were desperately unlucky not to pull off another one–two–three. Ernie Nott, having upped the lap record by no less than 5mph, was comfortably leading his team-mate Graham Walker

when a tappet locknut slackened on the last lap.

Spannerless, Nott had to hold the push-rod in position by hand, which dropped him to fourth place and let Ted Mellors' New Imperial into third, behind the Rudges of Walker and Tyrell Smith.

The most amazing aspect of the Lightweight one–two–three in 1934 was that the factory had pulled out of racing more than a year earlier, and Graham Walker had formed a private syndicate of riders. Fortunately, for 1934, he enlisted the dynamic, if ageing, talents of Jimmy Simpson, who delighted every soul on the Island by scoring his one and only TT win in 13 years of bitter hard luck.

For all George Hack's brilliance, the dominance of overhead camshafts in racing was inevitable. But, until their demise with the Second World War, Rudge cashed in on their successes with a string of roadsters, TT replicas and dirt-track machines, all based on the works models. The semi-radial Ulster survived to the end, not only with a five-bolt, light-alloy cylinder head, but also with such refinements as tubular aluminium pushrods, fully enclosed valves and a hand-operated centre stand.

It was as civilised a descendant as you could imagine of Graham Walker's history-making five-hundred.

Sunbeam Model 90

If the Brough Superior was the Rolls-Royce of motor cycles, then the single-cylinder Sunbeam, built by John Marston of Wolverhampton, was the Bentley, such was the quality of its engineering and black-and-gold finish. No one would credit the company with being fundamental innovators, though they were well to the fore in detail design. Rather than technical novelty, their hallmark was superlative workmanship allied to immaculate finish.

Right from the start they pioneered the oilbath chaincase, primary and secondary alike – a feature their motor cycles inherited from the pushbikes produced earlier.

In the beginning they made vee-twins and singles, both with side valves. Within the limitations imposed by the side-valve layout, their detail design was so good that they soon acquired a reputation for outstanding reliability.

Indeed, their first two TT victories – the Seniors of 1920 and 1922 – were achieved with side-valve engines. The 1920 event was won at record speed by Tommy de la Hay, with his team-mate George Dance setting the lap record. Two years later, Alec Bennett established both race and lap records.

In those early days, as in a later period when their overhead-valve models were second to none, the works racers were basically standard sports machines specially prepared. Unquestionably the most famous of those ohv singles was the 500cc (80 × 98 mm) Model 90 racer, on which the tiny but tough Charlie Dodson won the 1928 and 1929 Senior TTs, and which was also marketed in roadster guise as the Model 9.

Though the 350cc, 500cc and 600cc catalogue models of the time all had side valves, Sunbeam introduced overhead valves in about 1923, and George Dance established a truly formidable reputation in sprints with a bike capable of 90mph. The following year, the overhead-valver, in both 350cc and 500 cc sizes, made its mark in the European grands prix (although not in the TT) and

On the first of Sunbeam's overhead-valve five-hundreds, George Dance dominated British sprinting in 1923. Here he is at Harling, near Thetford

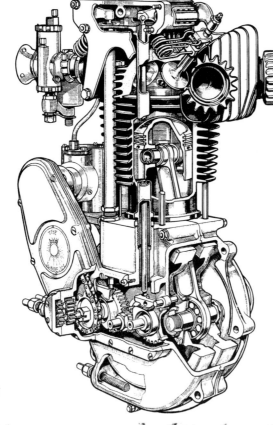

Right conventional but soundly designed, the Model 90 had long, hollow pushrods, double hairpin valve springs, massive exhaust finning and very effective flywheels

Below the short-lived overhead-camshaft engine of 1925, with single hairpin valve springs. Pushrods were re-adopted the following year

George Dance lifted the 350cc hour record to 80·24 miles, and the two-hour record to 70·52mph. Features of those 1924 machines included inclined pushrods, triple-coil valve springs and four speeds.

In 1925, Sunbeam were among the first to switch to an overhead camshaft and hairpin valve springs. Other features were double exhaust ports and dry-sump lubrication. But the cam form that had been evolved for pushrods, with their inevitable flexure, proved less suitable when that flexure was eliminated, and the racing machines reverted to pushrods for 1926.

That year's layout was to form the basis for the subsequent racing and sports models, with parallel pushrods, and Graham Walker foreshadowed the Model 90's winning reputation in the 500cc Ulster Grand Prix.

The following year he won the same class in the GP d'Europe, on the tortuous Nürburgring, while Dodson scooped the 350cc Ulster. The climax of Sunbeam racing successes was imminent, and it came in the summer of 1928, in the Isle of Man.

That year's Senior TT was run in such appalling weather that it was the slowest for four years. After a cautious start Dodson was no higher than fifth on the first lap and fourth on the second, but he moved into the lead on lap three and seemed a racing certainty to win.

On the sixth lap, however, his concentration was distracted by a waving spectator at Keppel Gate and he pranged. Unknown to Dodson, the 2½ minutes he lost as a result let Graham Walker (Rudge), an earlier starter, into the lead; Dodson was pleasantly surprised, nearly a lap later, to pass the broken-down Rudge on the Mountain Mile and go on to win – a feat he soon repeated in the Belgian and German GPs.

Just to emphasise that his TT victory owed precious little to luck, he repeated it in 1929, with record race and lap speeds, taking the lead on lap four after a careful start on wet roads. That year he followed up with wins in the French and Belgian GPs.

As mentioned, the works Model 90s were merely catalogue racers meticulously prepared, but Dodson's had also to be specially tailored to suit his stature. Dark, dapper and athletic, he scaled a mere 119lb. Under today's minimum-weight regulation, his machine would have had to carry a 13-lb lump of lead!

As it was, his saddle was a mere 15½in above the footrests, the handlebar grips only 19in forward of the saddle nose, and the kneegrips 12in ahead of the saddle cheeks.

But what he lacked in size and weight Dodson made up in strength and stamina, for he was a physical-culture fanatic.

His 1929 mount had a larger tank, and foot change instead of hand, but in other respects it was practically identical with the previous year's model, and it was the last pushrod two-valver to win the Senior TT. Conventional though the basic layout undoubtedly was, a lot of top-class engineering principles had been brought to bear on it.

At the top, the iron cylinder head had a thick section as a heat reservoir, and the deepest-ever cluster of cooling fins between the splayed exhaust ports. The hairpin-controlled valves were set at 90 degrees, while the 7·5:1 full-skirt piston, with its pronounced dome and valve pockets, had three plain rings, the lowest acting as an oil scraper in conjunction with a perforated chamfer below it.

At the bottom, a very stiff I-section characterised the connecting-rod, and the vast bulk of the flywheel mass was concentrated in the rims, where it had the most effect. Reaching right up from the pivoted cam followers to the overhead rockers, the long pushrods were hollow. In the dry-sump lubrication system, the double gear pump fed the big end, cams, rocker spindles and valve stems, and scavenged the crankcase.

Unusual on a TT machine was a quickly detachable rear wheel. The tyre valves were of Woods type (as used on pushbikes), and the breather in the top of the petrol tank was filled with sponge to prevent splashing when braking with a full tank.

Dodson's 1929 victories were the racing swansong of the engine type, but the catalogue racer – eventually the single-port Model 95L – was produced until 1935, mostly along with 350cc and 250cc versions, roadster equivalents and long-stroke side valve units.

The industrial upheavals of the period pushed Sunbeam under the banners of first ICI, then AMC and finally BSA. Design policy changed tremendously. With valve enclosure, high camshafts and plunger rear springing all helped make the later 'Beams so far removed from their predecessors as to be unrecognisable. Eventually a brief bid was made to restore the marque's prestige with the shaft-driven twin after the war.

With due respect to all these layouts, however, the glory of the name Sunbeam rests chiefly on the superb performances of the Model 90 in the hands of such masters as Charlie Dodson, George Dance and Alec Bennett.

Top *Arthur Simcock, Charlie Dodson (winner) and Alec Bennett – who took the manufacturers' team prize in the 1929 Senior TT*

Above *still winning – at the Nürburgring. Dr Helmut Krakowizer wins a 1973 vintage race on a 1929 Model 90*

Left *1931 version of the 500cc two-port roadster. Primary and final drives were on opposite sides*

59

Excelsior Mechanical Marvel

Combustion-chamber shape was one of the chief preoccupations of engine designers in the early 1930s. It was then widely thought that the nearest practical approach to the ideal was a hemisphere, despite the facts that the use of two large valves left insufficient room in the middle for the sparking plug, which had to be set to one side, and a really high compression ratio squeezed the gases into a horrid 'orange-peel' space.

In terms of volumetric efficiency (hence bhp/litre) motor cycles were at that time well ahead of cars, for most bikes had what in car parlance are now called part-spherical crossflow cylinder heads. Further, taking a tip from high-efficiency aircraft engine practice, motor-cycle designers were already exploring four-valve layouts.

Triumph and Rudge had long since designed engines with parallel pairs of valves. While that left room for the plug in the middle of the head (for the shortest flame path) it meant changing the head shape from part-spherical to pent roof.

Next, Rudge had scored overwhelming racing successes by setting four valves radially in a part-sphere and opening them through a complex system of six rockers (page 54). The plug was still central, the two exhaust ports were widely splayed, but there was only one carburettor, serving the two inlet valves through a divided port.

In 1933 Excelsior went the whole hog with a radial-valve two-fifty having completely separate inlet ports, too, each served by its own carburettor. Their approach to the problem of operating radial valves was entirely different from Rudge's, and led to the bike being immediately dubbed the Mechanical Marvel.

Made for Excelsior by Burney and Blackburne, the engine was designed by the B and B chief engineer, Ike Hatch, in collaboration with Excelsior's Eric Walker, who was also responsible for the rest of the bike. As with the Rudge design three years earlier, the radial-valve layout proved to be a recipe for instant success.

Almost straight from the drawing board, and in gale-force winds, the Mechanical Marvel was ridden to victory in the 1933 Lightweight TT by Sid Gleave, who set a record average of 71·59mph and made the fastest lap at 72·62mph.

In designing the valve gear, Hatch seemed to be at pains to avoid the awkward sort of

Sid Gleave on his way to victory in the 1933 Lightweight TT on the twin-carburettor Excelsior Mechanical Marvel

Gleave relaxes after his win. In front of his shin can be seen the magneto, skew-driven from the intermediate timing pinion

contact between the first and second rockers in the Rudge layout. Since the rocker spindles were at right angles to one another, that contact could be geometrically sound only if the surfaces were spherically ground, so reducing contact to a point.

Instead of one camshaft, as in the Rudge, Hatch used two – supported in ball bearings – across the front and rear of the very high crankcase mouth. Each cam operated a steeply inclined pushrod, at the top of which was a piston sliding in a bronze bush in the rocker housing. Side by side on the flat top of each piston, bore the inner ends of a pair of rockers, making rolling line contact.

Each rocker was supported on three roller bearings lubricated by grease gun, although the rocker boxes themselves, along with the big end, mains and cylinder wall, were fed with oil from the main supply. The valve guides were fed with a different grade of oil from a small compartment in the petrol tank.

Unlike the radial Rudge, the Mechanical Marvel had downdraught induction. The throttles were coupled through a junction box under the tank. Both slides normally worked in unison, but they could be arranged to open progressively, as in some twin-choke car carburettors.

At the bottom, the engine was up to date in having the well-supported mainshafts forged integrally with the flywheels. The Hiduminium connecting rod ran on an experimental, needle-roller big-end bearing,

while the 8·6:1 piston (also a Hiduminium forging) had three $\frac{1}{16}$ in-thick plain rings.

Cylinder head and barrel alike were clamped to the crankcase by four long bolts reaching right down to the main bearings. The BTH magneto was driven by skew gears from the intermediate timing pinion. Transmission was through an Albion four-speed gearbox, and one of the bikes (Sid Crabtree's) had interconnected brakes, another Rudge spin-off.

Indeed, so experimental were the TT machines that individual engines differed in several details. And Wal Handley, one of the official team, hedged his bet by making a personal entry on a Moto-Guzzi.

Handley's Mechanical Marvel led, by a mere second, on the first lap, before Gleave took over the running. And Wal was eventually robbed of second place by engine failure at Sulby on the last lap.

Although the winning engine stripped to perfection, many changes were made for 1934. Bowden carburettors (with butterfly throttles) supplanted the Amals. The big-end bearing was modified and the connecting rod lengthened (also the cylinder to suit). One way and another, in spite of increased petrol and oil capacities, 30lb was slashed off the machine's weight, so both handling and braking were improved.

For all that, the previous year's successes were not repeated and Gleave finished no higher than sixth in the Lightweight TT, way behind the radial Rudges that scooped

On this machine, the Amal carburettors have been replaced by Bowdens with butterfly throttles. The rev-counter is driven by the exhaust camshaft

The exhaust pushrod tube can be seen sloping up from the crankcase mouth. In the housing at the top, a piston operated the adjacent ends of the two rockers

the first three places. Moreover, the engine proved tricky to maintain and tune.

In desperation, Excelsior turned to an orthodox, bevel-driven-ohc, two-valve Manxman for 1935, but that was no better. So, for 1936, they crossed the two engines and the offspring had an aluminium-bronze head with a single overhead camshaft operating four valves through six Rudge-type rockers. It came in two sizes – a two-fifty, on which Tyrell Smith and Ginger Wood finished second in the 1936 and 1937 Lightweight TTs respectively, and a three-fifty that brought Tyrell Smith home seventh in the 1937 Junior.

For all their ingenuity, the bikes were no faster than the two-valvers and less reliable, so Excelsior settled for orthodoxy from then on. In any case, design and development in the 250cc field were so diversified during that period that six different engine types were used by the winners of the last seven pre-war Lightweight TTs.

Those types were: twin-carb four-valve (Gleave's 1933 Excelsior); single-carb four-valve (Jimmy Simpson's 1934 Rudge); ohc two-valve (Stanley Woods' and Omobono Tenni's Moto-Guzzis in 1935 and 1937 respectively); pushrod two-valve (Bob Foster's 1936 New Imperial); supercharged two-stroke (Ewald Kluge's 1938 DKW); and double-knocker two-valve (Ted Mellor's 1939 Benelli).

The four-valve engine languished until Honda put it back on the map so emphatically in 1961 with Mike Hailwood's record-shattering wins in the 250cc TT and the 125cc TT.

Husqvarna vee-twin

Even in the 1930s, it was obvious to any knowledgeable engineer that the single-cylinder engine must eventually give way to the multi, for this had the advantages of sheer power (from higher peak rpm) and smoother torque (more frequent power impulses). The fact that the single held on as long as it did was largely due to the talents of some notable British designers and development engineers, and to the fact that public demand then, as now, was strongly influenced by racing achievements.

The first type of multi to knock the racing single off its perch was the vee-twin, when Stanley Woods won the 1935 Senior TT by four seconds on a 120-degree Moto-Guzzi. But Husqvarna, in Sweden, had already done much of the vee-twin donkey work, though with an engine with a more conventional cylinder angle of 50 degrees.

Indeed, in the previous year Woods'

Senior Husky had plainly chalked the writing on the wall. In foul weather, not only did he make the fastest lap of 80·49mph but for more than 6¾ wet, misty, slippery laps – although unable to catch the great Jimmy Guthrie on the number-one Norton – he comfortably held off the challenge of Guthrie's meteoric team-mate Jimmy Simpson, in spite of stepping off and remounting at Ramsey Hairpin. But then, as Woods started the final mountain descent only eight miles from the finish, the Husky tank ran dry and the Swedish factory was robbed of the glory of splitting the two 'invincible' Nortons.

It would have been more than a well-deserved climax to the week for Husqvarna. Four days earlier, Ernie Nott – tough as nails but not so talented as Woods – had struggled through to third place in the Junior behind Guthrie and Simpson. And

Despite oil on the rear tyre and a persistent misfire, Ernie Nott holds third place in the 1934 Junior TT, when he was beaten only by two of the invincible works Nortons

The Husqvarna vee-twin had a conventional cylinder angle of 50 degrees. Light alloy was used extensively

Two Montlhéry grand-prix winners in 1935. On the left is Raegenholm on the victorious 350cc Husqvarna

that despite persistent misfiring out of corners and lurid slides caused by oil from the timing cover leaking on to the right-hand side of the rear tyre.

That there were any Huskies in the Island at all that year was well-nigh incredible and a tremendous tribute to the dedication of the racing staff. For on the last Saturday in May, as a giant crane swung a lorry full of precious raceware from the Gothenburg quayside towards the ship's hold, a cable broke, one wheel slipped off the sling, and the lorry crashed upside down on the quayside, spilling bikes in all directions.

Engineer Folke Mannerstedt and Sweden's two star riders, Ragnar Sunnqvist and Gunnar Kalen, were almost in tears as they surveyed bent frames, forks and wheels, dented tanks and at least one smashed engine. The wreckage was rushed back to the factory, where night-and-day repair work

eventually got some bikes to the Island, albeit late. That was not the end of Husqvarna's troubles. For Sunnqvist contracted appendicitis and was forbidden to ride.

When the machines did arrive in the Island, they were the focus of all eyes. For Mannerstedt had worked wonders on them during the winter, and they had already dominated the Swedish TT even more than usual. Switching to light allow wherever he could – including the connecting rods, cylinders and heads, tanks and cone hubs – he had slashed the dry weight from 347lb to 274lb.

This 73lb saving had boosted acceleration and braking tremendously. Capable of 118 mph, the five-hundreds were just about the fastest bikes in the Island, while the three-fifties were among the quickest Juniors. And the girder forks had grown AJS-type snubber springs to tame the handling.

Bad luck continued to dog the team during practice. Woods hit a sheep at Ballig and broke the front down tube. Nott found the three-fifty still frisky, and sheets of flame from the exhausts during acceleration showed a carburation flat spot.

After surviving the calamities of the TT venture so courageously, the team contested the remaining European grands prix – where Sunnqvist and Kalen were persistent thorns in the flesh of the winning five-hundreds, and Nott was usually second best only to Simpson in the 350cc class.

Although Husqvarna gave the TT a miss in 1935, they hit the headlines elsewhere. On the very fast Avus track in Berlin, Sunnqvist beat Karl Gall on the works supercharged BMW. At Saxtorp, Woods won the Swedish Grand Prix. For the third year running, S. Edlund won the Swedish TT (a different event). And throughout the second half of the season Sunnqvist continued to harass the all-conquering works Nortons.

But the Swedish factory's racing programme was on the decline. Exhaust megaphones were adopted in 1936, but development generally was in a minor key, with a stay to steady the float chambers, and tank-side shields for the air intakes.

New to the TT course that year, Sunnqvist could manage only 16th in the Junior and had brake trouble in the Senior. In any case, he could no longer spare the time for a full racing programme. By that time the super-stars were all tied to the leading British, German and Italian teams.

But in six years of classic racing the Swedes had shown the proud singles which way the wind was blowing, and with a layout that

Thirty years after the war ended his racing career, Stanley Woods opens the 1969 Anderstorp race meeting in Sweden with a demonstration ride on a 1935 three-fifty

Close-up of the 350cc engine, showing the crankcase stiffening, hairpin valve springs, carburettor intake shield and float-chamber steady

was largely contentional, too. Almost the only novelties on the original 1931 500cc version were hairpin valve springs, carburettors with vertical intakes, and (instead of the usual tank rail) a pair of splayed tubes from the top of the front down tube to the seat stays.

The engine was a long-stroke (65 × 75mm) with pushrod valve operation, front and rear exhausts, a modest cr (7·3:1) and a chain-driven Bosch magneto. The four-speed gear-box was controlled by a rocking pedal.

With 9·5:1 compression, modification of the induction layout, stiffening of the crank-case, enclosure of the valve gear and lubrica-tion of the guides, the engine soon out-stripped the frame in performance. If the handling had really been tamed, and if the Swedes had had the strength in depth of the star-studded Norton team, then Husqvarna rather than Moto-Guzzi might have de-throned the big single.

Matchless Silver Hawk

Two overhead-camshaft fours of outstanding technical merit – the Ariel Square Four and the Matchless Silver Hawk – burst on the British scene at the London Show in the autumn of 1930. To a public previously fed on a diet predominantly of singles, with a sprinkling of flat twins and vee-twins, it was difficult to decide which of the two new-comers was the more exciting.

The Square Four survived and evolved for more than a quarter-century, whereas the Hawk died, substantially unchanged, after only five years (and a total production of 500 to 550). Yet the Matchless seemed to have the initial edge: not only was the engine larger – 600cc against 500cc – but the Hawk was advertised as the only four in the world with rear springing. What's more, it had a single crankshaft, with two throws set at 180 degrees, whereas the Ariel had two 180-degree crankshafts coupled by gears which could not be entirely quietened and were reckoned expensive.

Those with crystal-ball minds might have anticipated the Silver Hawk, with its narrow-angle, double-vee cylinder arrangement. For only a year earlier Matchless had launched the Silver Arrow – a 400cc narrow-angle vee-twin, with side valves, that proved to be something of a guinea pig.

Although the Hawk's valve operation was completely different, the engine was in many ways a doubled-up Arrow.

Designed by Charlie Collier, one of the Matchless founders, the Arrow had the 54×86mm cylinders cast in an iron monobloc with an included angle of only 26 degrees. The exhaust ports faced to the right, where they were coupled by a cast-iron manifold with a forward outlet for the pipe. Bolted to a flange on the left side of the block, a single carburettor fed a transverse passage which branched out to serve both inlet valves.

Lying fore and aft in a compartment in the right-hand half of the crankcase, the camshaft was driven by skew gears from the end of the crankshaft. A coupling at the rear end of the camshaft drove a Lucas Magdyno situated above the three-speed Sturmey Archer gearbox. At $\frac{7}{16}$in, the pitch of the single-strand primary chain was a novelty. In the dry-sump lubrication system, the four-pint tank was bolted to the front of the crankcase to catch some air.

Pivoted on Silentbloc bonded-rubber bushes, the rear fork was fully triangulated, the apex operating a pair of barrel-shape coil springs under the saddle, with a friction-damper knob on each side.

Engine overheating led to deeper head

For all its zip, the Matchless Silver Hawk was exceptionally quiet and comfortable to ride. The primary chain was automatically tensioned by spring-loaded flexible steel strips in the top and bottom of the case. As on the Silver Arrow, the cylinder block and head were monobloc castings, with the carburettor on the left. The centre main bearing made stripping and rebuilding the crankcase assembly a tricky job

Virtually a guinea pig for the 600cc overhead-camshaft vee-four Silver Hawk, the Matchless Silver Arrow – a 400cc side-valve, 26-degree vee-twin – had a flat-face cylinder-head casting. Both brakes were operated by the right-side pedal and there was an auxiliary handlebar lever for the front one only

finning for 1931, when four speeds were standardised, too. But quiet and docile though the Arrow undoubtedly was, it never became popular and lasted only four years. Simply, it was heavy and gutless – and not many riders were prepared to fork out £55 for mediocre performance.

How to combine the party manners of the Arrow with really zippy acceleration and a top speed of more than 80mph was a problem tackled by Bert Collier, Charlie's brother. His solution bristled with novelties.

In laying out the Hawk, Bert decided to retain many Arrow features, such as the rear springing, coupled brakes, oil-tank position and an instrument panel atop the handlebar.

The novelties included a centre bearing for the crankshaft, coil ignition, four speeds, an induction layout giving an equal length of tract for all cylinders, a comprehensive oiling system, and a more-or-less oval shape for the cylinder heads. Also, the bore and stroke (50·8 × 73mm) were both smaller than in the Arrow. And the primary drive had fixed centres, with the $\frac{3}{8}$in duplex chain automatically tensioned and running in oil.

The built-up crankshaft, which had heavy enough cheeks and bobweights to need no separate flywheel, was supported in a long phosphor-bronze bush in each crankcase half, and a roller bearing in a steel plate clamped between the two.

Air space was provided round each cylinder in the block casting. And the head shape (along with the matching top of the cylinder bores) had to be made oval to accommodate two $1\frac{1}{16}$in-diameter parallel valves in a bore size of only 2in. Compression ratio was 6·1:1.

On the right, two pairs of bevel gears and a vertical shaft (with two Oldham couplings) drove the camshaft.

A skew gear on the vertical shaft, just above the bottom level, drove the rear-mounted dynamo and distributor through a rubber coupling. Firing order was: front right, rear right, front left, rear left.

Another skew gear, inboard of the crankshaft bevel, drove the oil pump, in which the plunger both rotated and reciprocated. One oil feed went direct to the plain main bearings and big ends; another went, via a tell-tale in the instrument panel, to the top bevel box. From there, it overflowed into a camshaft trough and on to the eight straight rockers. From the drain to the sump some of the oil was diverted, through a needle-controlled bypass, to the primary chain.

In the 12-bolt head, the transverse induction passage from the carburettor went to the centre of a cross-shaped network branching to the four inlet valves. But the claim for perfect distribution is debatable, since the charge for the left-hand cylinders had to turn through a far sharper angle than that for the right. At the front and rear of the head, cast-iron manifolds coupled the exhaust ports, to feed single pipes on the right, which led to a common silencer.

Bert Collier's aims were seen to be achieved when the Hawk bettered 80mph, yet would dawdle in top gear at a fast walking pace. So effortlessly did the 26bhp engine start that it could be done by hand, and it idled well. It could be decoked in the frame.

But, as with the Arrow, the cylinder head overheated when the bike was really flogged, though the air spaces round the manifolds were enlarged. Moreover, the bevels were prone to whine (if too tightly meshed) or rattle (if too slack).

For all its ingenuity and charms, it proved too expensive – £75 in 1931, £78 10s in 1935. By the time it was phased out after five years, its manufacturers had learned, as have many others, that there are more customers for cheap performance than there are for expensive refinement.

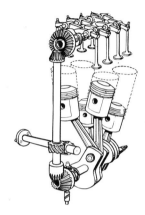

Layout of the Silver Hawk engine. To keep the front and rear cylinder bores in line, the con-rod big-end eyes were slightly offset, with one row of rollers to each eye. The two-to-one reduction in the camshaft drive was confined to the top pair of bevels – no hunting tooth to spread wear

Moto-Guzzi vee-twin

Of the extraordinary variety of Moto-Guzzis that made such a tremendous impact on classic racing over a quarter of a century, the 500cc 120-degree vee-twin stands out on two counts. First, for the sensational way in which it sounded the death-knell of both the big single-cylinder engine and the unsprung frame, when Stanley Woods humiliated the hauty works Nortons and beat Jimmy Guthrie by four seconds in the 1935 Senior TT. Then 16 years later – with the big single enjoying its final fling and multis such as the AJS Porcupine twin and Gilera and MV Agusta fours all on the way up – the 120-degree Moto-Guzzi proved it was still competitive by trouncing them all on the drenched and tricky 4½-mile Bremgarten circuit in Berne, where Fergus Anderson won the 1951 Swiss Grand Prix by nearly two minutes.

Years before 1935, imaginative engineers had been predicting the eventual superiority of the multi-cylinder engine. But Joe Craig's passionate dedication to the single had developed it to such a pitch that the big Norton had dominated the 500cc class so emphatically and for so long as to seem utterly invincible.

Similarly with frames. Rear springing must come, said the pundits, just as it had on cars long, long since. But many previous examples of motor-cycle rear springing had been conversions or attachments that lacked lateral rigidity and so gave the idea a bad name by impairing handling. Moreover, the steering geometry and weight distribution of the works Nortons had been systematically improved to the point where their handling was a byword, so that rear springing seemed both unnecessary and undesirable.

The original Moto-Guzzi vee-twin was virtually the factory's flat single with an extra cylinder squeezed in beneath the saddle. Tubes alongside the wheel housed the rear suspension springs

In retrospect, it seems strange that nobody foresaw Stanley Woods' record-splintering Senior TT victory in 1935, for only three days earlier, in the Lightweight event, he had made mincemeat of the four-valve Rudges that had swamped the previous year's race – and the flat single on which he did that was virtually the Senior machine without the rear cylinder.

For compact installation, that cylinder fitted snugly between the crankcase and the saddle. Separate crankpins were used, to give even firing intervals, and since the pins were integral with the crank webs, the roller big-end bearings were split diametrically, an unusual practice. In typical Moto-Guzzi fashion, the flywheel was outside, on the left, and the gearbox was in unit with the crankcase. The overhead camshafts were bevel driven, hairpin springs were used for the valves, and the magneto was between the cylinder bases. Since the cylinders and their heads were made of cast iron, the machine was on the heavy side, at 375lb. A wedge-shape oil tank topped the petrol tank and carried the chin pad.

Just as unorthodox as the engine was the rear springing, for the fork was triangulated *below* the pivot point, and controlled by long springs in horizontal tubes slung low on both sides of the wheel. Damping was by friction discs, and the pressure on them was adjustable by a lever on the left side of the tank.

Because of atrocious weather, with the mountain section of the course completely blanketed in mist, the race was postponed for a day. When it did get going, all the early signs were that Jimmy Guthrie was going to dominate it on the number one Norton as he had the previous year. For Woods made a slowish start and by the end of six laps, with only one to go, he lagged 26 seconds behind the Norton ace. Such a deficit seemed far too great for even the great Stanley to make up in a single lap.

But there was a foretaste of the drama to come when Woods – despite feverish activity in his pit suggesting a second stop for fuel – gambled and screamed through non-stop. By that time Guthrie, a much earlier starter, was more than half way round his final lap. Indeed, when he finished he was acclaimed the winner, for nobody imagined Woods could peg back so much time, even if his petrol lasted out.

But Stanley was riding as never before. Revving the willing engine to the limit, he not only hoisted the lap record to 86·53mph;

Airborne at Ballaugh Bridge in the 1949 Senior TT is Bob Foster, who was leading on the 'Red Devil' when the clutch failed near the end

Notable developments on this 1950 model include down-draught induction, leading-link front fork (with parallelogram brake anchorage), form-fitting tank, large-diameter frame spine and cantilever rear suspension

In atrocious conditions, Fergus Anderson beat far more modern designs in winning the 1951 Swiss Grand Prix by nearly two minutes

he also made up enough time to set a record speed for the race (84·68mph) and to pip Guthrie by four seconds. Those four seconds made history, for they signalled that the big single and rigid frame were on their way out.

After the war, it was not only Fergus Anderson's 1951 Swiss GP victory that proved how far ahead of its time the 120-degree Moto-Guzzi had been. Two years earlier, Bob Foster was unlucky not to scoop another Senior TT with the red devil (as it was nicknamed). True, the machine had been updated, with a leading-link front fork and improvements to the brakes and rear springing. But it was basically the same, and Foster soon took command of the race.

On the opening lap he lay fourth, 20 seconds behind Les Graham and Ted Frend (who tied for the lead of the AJS Porcupines), with Harold Daniell sandwiched in third spot on a works Norton. With the fastest lap of the race, Foster then hoisted himself to third on the tail of the Porcs, after which he

pulled relentlessly ahead and led Graham by no less thn 57 seconds at the end of lap five. Alas for Foster, the clutch packed up on lap six – and the race eventually went to Daniell.

Foster tried his luck again in 1950, but could manage only a steady sixth for five laps before a minute's tinkering, again at Sulby, put him farther out of the picture, the race going comfortably to Norton's brilliant new superstar, Geoff Duke.

There was no doubting the Moto-Guzzi's superiority in Berne the following May. With the TT next in the calendar, the works teams were there in force for a dress rehearsal. The 127-mile race was run in such teeming rain that many of the 25 starters wore oilskins over their leathers, but the tricky conditions showed up the Moto-Guzzi's stability to fine advantage, and Anderson led the pack first time round, chased by Georges Cordey and Geoff Duke (Nortons), Les Graham (MV Agusta) and Reg Armstrong (AJS Porcupine).

A couple of laps later, Duke and Anderson were mixing it so keenly up front that the rest were well in arrears. Then Duke's magneto went dead, Graham threw his MV up the road, and Anderson found himself way, way ahead of the other works Norton, in spite of easing the pace. Shortly before half-distance, Cordey's mag went the way of Duke's, and Armstrong got the best of the cut and thrust for runner-up spot. By then only 14 riders survived, most lapped by Anderson.

Armstrong hung on to his second place to the end, though he finished best part of a lap in arrears. And, as the rain stopped towards the end, Anderson's team-mate Enrico Lorenzetti put on a spurt to give Moto-Guzzi third place, too. Truly, the 120-degree vee-twin from Mandello del Lario, on the eastern shore of Lake Como, was one of racing's classics.

Triumph Speed Twin

Extremists have long regarded the four-stroke parallel twin, with side-by-side crank-pins, either as the answer to a motor cyclist's prayer or as a mobile vibro-massage machine. But when, in the face of the single's 30-year dominance, Triumph boldly set the ball rolling in 1938 by marketing Edward Turner's 500cc Speed Twin, that model was destined to influence the evolution of touring and sports machines more than any other model before or since. It was an immediate success, and no sooner had the industry got back into its stride after the Second World War than most other British factories jumped smartly on the bandwagon.

Motor cyclists are notoriously conservative, and there is little doubt the Speed Twin's prospects were enhanced by its apparent resemblance to a two-port single, as well as by its neatness. More positively in its favour was the fact that the new engine slotted easily into the familiar Tiger 90 frame and the same gearbox, hubs and front fork could be used. Surprisingly, at 365lb the Speed Twin was 5lb lighter than the Tiger 90, while at £75 it was only £5 dearer.

Edward Turner, who probably had a greater flair for the commercial market than for engineering, joined Triumph in 1936 after leaving Ariel, where he had created the Square Four (page 41). But his Speed Twin was by no means the first parallel twin made by Triumph. Four years earlier there was the 650cc (70×84mm) Model 6/1 (also with the pistons in step) designed by Val Page. Advanced for its day, it had semi-unit construction of the engine and four-speed gearbox, with double-helical primary drive (the one-piece crankshaft ran backward). Robust and remarkably reliable, it earned Harry Perrey a sidecar Gold Medal in the 1933 International Six Days Trial. But it was too bulky and (at £75 15s) too expensive for commercial success.

Start of an era. The 1938 500cc Speed Twin, with tank-top instrument panel. To riders accustomed to twin-port singles, it didn't look too unconventional

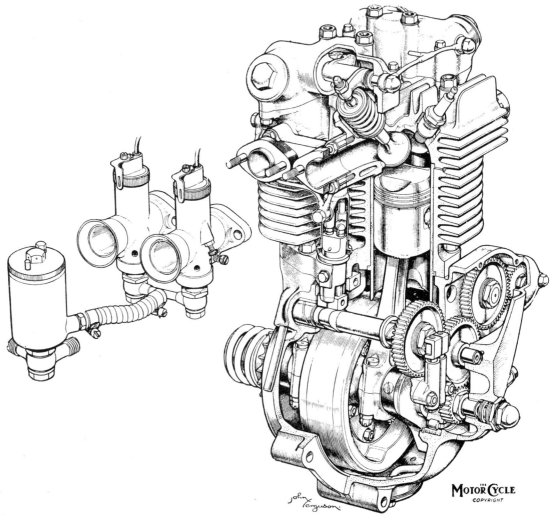

The engine of the Grand Prix racer, introduced in 1948, comprised a Tiger 100 bottom half and the light-alloy cylinder block and head from a wartime generator unit

Even 20 years before that there was a 600cc side-valve Triumph parallel twin, with a 180-degree forged crankshaft. Cylinder block and head were an integral iron casting, with the exhaust valves at the front and the inlets at the rear, all operated from a central camshaft driven by skew gears from the middle of the crankshaft. That model's chances of going into production were killed by the First World War.

Turner's confidence in reviving the parallel-twin layout was based on its smoother torque, better low-speed pulling and acceleration, the more agreeable nature of its running and the fact that it was much easier to silence. He also claimed that its engine balance was the same as that of a single. This claim, however, was based on theory, and was not borne out in practice, because of the twin's whippier crankshaft, in conjunction with the wider spacing of its main bearings and their less rigid support.

That original Speed Twin engine had a one-piece iron cylinder block (63 × 80mm) with a six-stud base flange (soon thickened and changed to eight studs). The head was also a one-piece iron casting. Running in

ball main bearings of $2\frac{3}{4}$in outside diameter, the cranks were flanged at their inner ends for bolting to the central flywheel. Forged in RR56 aluminium alloy, the connecting rods ran direct on the crank journals, while the steel caps were lined with white metal. Full-skirt pistons gave a compression ratio of 7·2:1.

In bronze-bushed tunnels at the front and rear of the crankcase mouth, the gear-driven camshafts actuated large-radius followers in cast-iron guides. Chromium-plated tubes enclosed the duralumin pushrods, which operated forged rockers in bolted-on light-alloy boxes. Behind the cylinders, the Magdyno was gear-driven from the inlet camshaft, while a peg on the end of the shaft drove the double-plunger oil pump. Peak engine power was claimed to be 26bhp at 6000rpm and top speed, chin on tank, was about 90 mph.

Only a year after the launch of the Speed Twin came the Tiger 100 – an £80 sports version, with polished ports and innards, and forged slipper pistons boosting compression to 8:1. For £5 extra, there was the option of an aluminium-bronze cylinder head. The

Ready for the 1949 International Six Days Trial – a Trophy model, with siamesed and upswept exhaust

On the Tiger 110 he shared with Dan Shorey, Mike Hailwood heads for victory in the 1958 Motor Cycle 500-miler at Thruxton

speed potential of the Triumph engine – amply proved on the drag strips since the Second World War – was first shown in 1939, when Ivan Wicksteed clapped on a blower and raised the Brooklands 500cc lap record to 118·02mph. Then Freddie Clarke, chief of the experimental department, bored out a Tiger 100 to 502cc and took the 750cc record at exactly the same speed.

In the long years since the war, Edward Turner's Speed Twin has spawned many descendants, ranging from 350cc (originally a prototype Army lightweight) through 650 to 750cc. First of the six-fifties was the Thunderbird, catalogued from 1950 to 1966.

It was introduced with a flourish when, late in September 1949, the first three production models were taken to Montlhéry, near Paris. There Alex Scobie, Bob Manns, Alan Jefferies, Jimmy Alves and Len Bayliss thrashed them round the concrete bowl at an average of 90mph for 500 miles, each bike signing off with a ton lap. Three years later, when an SU carburettor was standardised, Triumph staged a vastly different stunt and five riders, including Edward Turner, lapped a 10-mile road circuit at a steady 30mph – and averaged 155mpg.

Hotter versions of the six-fifty were the Tiger 110 (with pivoted rear fork) – on

which Dan Shorey and the up-and-coming
Mike Hailwood won the *Motor Cycle* 500-
miler at Thruxton in 1958 – and the twin-
carb Bonneville. That model was named
after Bill Johnson's American Class C record
of 147·32mph, when he rode a souped-up
Tiger 110 on the Bonneville Salt Flats in the
autumn of 1958. (Class C is for 650cc
stock machines). With 46bhp at 6500rpm in
standard trim, the Bonnie was enormously
successful in production-machine racing,
especially after Doug Hele brought his
experience and wizardry to the factory, and
vastly improved the steering and broadened
the power band. Among the Bonnie's more
outstanding successes were the 750cc Production Machine TT in 1967 (John Hartle)
and 1969 (Malcolm Uphill), and the *Motor
Cycle* 500-miler, at Brands Hatch in 1967 and
Thruxton in 1969.

Doug Hele was also responsible for the
50-bhp five-hundreds on which Gary Nixon
and Buddy Elmore swamped the 1967
Daytona 200, blowing off the mighty Harley-
Davidson seven-fifties with more than a lap
to spare (Elmore had chalked the writing on
the wall by winning the previous year's
event).

An out-and-out road racer – the 500cc
Grand Prix – was introduced in 1948, after
Ernie Lyons had won the wet and misty
Senior Manx GP on a prototype two years
earlier. Basically, the engine comprised a
Tiger 100 bottom half, topped by the square-
finned, light-alloy block and head from a
wartime generator unit. Front fork was
telescopic and the rear wheel was mounted

on the patented sprung hub. There was no
doubting the Grand Prix's speed, although
the handling could be hairy. But its engine
vibration was destructive and, though it won
plenty of minor races, it lacked the stamina
for serious events such as the TT.

About the same time (at the 1948 London
Show) Triumph brought out one of their
most successful five-hundreds – the TR5
Trophy, which had just cleaned up the
ISDT at San Remo, in Italy, winning both
the Trophy and Vase, besides one of the two
manufacturers' team prizes. As on the Grand
Prix, there was a Tiger 100 bottom half and
the square block and head. But there was
only one carburettor and the cams were
docile.

Versatility was the TR5's trump card and,
by ringing the changes on cams, pistons and
gear clusters, it could be made eminently
suitable for trials, scrambles, clubman racing
or commuting. When, in 1957, the 650cc
TR6 Trophy was introduced, it was anything but an enlarged TR5. Rather was it a
single-carb version of the Bonneville – and
very pleasant to boot. But the 500cc maid-of-
all-work lived on in the Adventurer.

The post-war history of the parallel-twin
four-stroke embraces many other makes, and
various attempts to tame engine vibration –
such as the AJS and Matchless middle main
bearing and Yamaha's Omni-Phase balancing system. (Triumph's own answer was to go
to three cylinders for 750cc upward.) Cock-
sure he may have been, but even Edward
Turner could never have guessed just what
his original Speed Twin would give rise to.

BMW Twins

Enthusiasts whose recollections reach back no farther than 1954 might feel that BMW's tremendous fame rests on two distinct achievements. First, the phenomenal dominance of their double-ohc transverse flat twins in the world sidecar championship and the Sidecar TT, not to mention the sidecar speed record. Second, the consistent production of a range of superlative shaft-driven, pushrod-ohv roadsters with a unique blend of high performance and impeccable manners which has instilled the utmost pride and joy into riders all over the world.

But those with longer memories may recall that BMW first hit the sporting jackpot, with supercharged solos, before the Second World War, and that the Munich factory's production of highly refined roadsters dates from way back in 1923, when Max Friz, debarred from continuing to design aircraft engines by the Versailles Treaty, switched his talents to motor cycles.

First of more than half-a-million. The original BMW flat twin – the 1923 three-speed 500cc side-valve R32 – had the traditional transverse cylinders, integral gearbox and shaft drive

One that got away. This exotic 1935 design never got into production

Scenes from Ernst Henne's eight years as a record breaker. Above with *streamlined helmet and tail, during a 750cc record bid near Vienna in 1931.* Top right *the following spring he prepares to break the flying-kilo record there.* Right *this cutaway shell shows the layout of the 500cc streamliner on which he averaged 174mph in 1937*

Apparently he was reluctant to make the change and had to be tempted by what, in those lean times, was the sheer luxury of a stove in his drawing office. No investment could have been more productive than that stove. For Friz's first design – the 500cc side-valve, three-speed shaft-drive R32 – was so far advanced as to be the sensation of the Paris Show. It was also the recognisable sire of the half-million basically similar machines that poured out of the factory in the following half-century to establish and maintain an unsurpassed reputation for top-quality design and engineering.

With Ernst Henne as the intrepid rider, BMW first inscribed their name in the record book one mid-September morning in 1929. Riding a partially faired, supercharged version of the newly catalogued ohv seven-fifty (virtually an overbored five-hundred), he streaked along the Munich–Ingolstadt autobahn at a mean speed of 135mph for the flying mile. In the next eight years he bagged no fewer than 76 world records, finishing up by robbing Piero Taruffi (Gilera) of the pre-

war fastest ever, with 174mph on a five-hundred.

During that spell, Henne waged a ding-dong battle for the flying-kilometre record with Britain's top speedsters, Joe Wright (OEC Temple) and Eric Fernihough (Brough Superior). Forfeiting 250cc to the British 1000cc vee-twins, Henne took a firm hold on the record, raising his speed by stages from 137·66mph in 1930 to 159·1mph in 1935.

The following year he rubbed salt into the British wounds by cutting his engine capacity to 500cc, yet sticking all of 10mph on to his speed with the aid of an all-enveloping shell. Six months later Ferni accepted the challenge, took his big Brough to Gyon, in Hungary, but could better Henne's speed by only $\frac{3}{4}$mph.

After a further six months Taruffi had a go, riding his enclosed and supercharged 500cc Gilera four on the Brescia–Bergamo autostrada. But though he was the first to top 170mph, he bettered Ferni's speed by even less than Ferni had bettered Henne's.

Left *in 1929, the first blown BMW had the supercharger driven by the magneto shaft, above the gearbox.*

Below left *Georg Meier airborne on Bray Hill during his record-breaking win in the 1939 Senior TT.*

Below *front view of Meier's 68-bhp blown flat twin, showing the carburettor intake shield*

The world had to wait no longer than five weeks for the German's reply. On the Frankfurt–Munich autobahn he averaged an arrogant 174mph, to put the record beyond reach until Wilhelm Herz shattered it on a blown NSU twin 14 years and a world war later.

In classic road racing, BMW were first to exploit supercharging to get on top of the five-hundred class, by vanquishing the almighty works Nortons and the Moto-Guzzi and Husqvarna vee-twins. With the car-burettor feeding into the top right, the Zoller eccentric-vane blower was built neatly on to the front of the crankcase. From the outlet at the bottom, the long induction pipes curved under the cylinders to the rear-facing inlet ports. Boost pressure was about 15psi.

What finally gave the machine its decisive edge was the adoption, in 1935, of double overhead camshafts, and the first-ever hydraulically damped telescopic front fork, followed shortly afterwards by plunger rear springing. From then on, BMW's classic

successes were no longer confined to Continental wins by Otto Ley and Karl Gall. The threat to Norton supremacy crossed the English Channel and, indeed, the Irish Sea.

Jock West marked BMW's Isle of Man debut with sixth place in the 1937 Senior TT, then won the Ulster Grand Prix. The following year, he improved to fifth in the Senior and repeated his Ulster win. The climax came in 1939, when Georg Meier, riding in only his second TT, gave a masterly display on his 68-bhp, 140-mph machine to dominate the Senior, ably backed up by West in second place.

For a month or two more, Meier was unbeatable – until Dorino Serafini, on the blown Gilera four, put his nose out of joint by getting the upper hand in the Swedish and German GPs, then relieving Meier of the European 500cc championship.

After the Second World War, with super-charging outlawed for classic road racing, BMW never again got to the top of the solo tree, their best Senior TT performance being Walter Zeller's fourth place in 1956 (also in only his second IoM ride), in spite of over-

gearing as a result of a last-minute decision to dispense with the fairing. But the factory's switch from their brief solo supremacy before the war to their long sidecar dominance after it illustrates the much greater suitability of the engine layout for sidecar racing.

In an outfit, as distinct from a solo, engine width is no disadvantage in cornering. Indeed, it can be slung ultra-low to facilitate drifting in both directions. The jutting cylinders are beautifully placed for cooling, the vibrationless running is a boon and the shaft drive ideally suited to the arduous duty.

The proof of all this is in the world-championship and TT statistics. Since 1954 BMW drivers have monopolised the sidecar championship, except for two years. In 1968 the incredible Helmut Fath, who first took the title on a BMW outfit eight years earlier, won it again on his home-built Urs four (see page 157). In 1971 Horst Owesle repeated the impertinence on the same outfit.

When the 500cc Sidecar TT was revived in 1954, Eric Oliver's swansong victory on a Norton was to herald an absolute avalanche of BMW wins, achieved under the technical

BMWs best post-war solo TT performance was Walter Zeller's fourth place in the 1956 Senior, despite over-gearing. Here he is on the mountain section

Above *Wilhelm Noll
setting the record lap in the
1954 Sidecar TT. He
crashed when leading a few
miles from the finish*

Left *later that year, Noll
became the world's fastest
sidecarrist, achieving
174mph on this fully
streamlined outfit*

guidance of Dipl Ing Alex von Falkenhausen. Only in 1962 did they falter. For Florian Camathias pranged at Kerrowmoar when leading on lap two, then Max Deubel's engine seized at Ballig when he, too, was leading on the third and final lap, leaving Chris Vincent a surprised and comparatively slow winner on a BSA outfit.

The names of the BMW drivers who have put their trust in the five-speed German power plant, to swell the lists of world champions and TT winners, reads like a who's-who of all-time sidecar greats. One of them, Wilhelm Noll, made a few out-of-season dashes along the Munich–Ingolstadt autobahn in November 1955 to become the fastest sidecarrist ever, achieving 174mph with his machine completely enclosed.

Yet, except for the use of direct petrol injection early on, there is little in the engine that is out of the ordinary. Perhaps the most surprising feature is the use of conventional valve rockers in conjunction with double overhead camshafts. This is because the bevel drive goes straight to the exhaust shaft on the right and the inlet shaft on the left, and the other camshafts are geared directly to them. Hence the camshafts are much closer together than the valve tips.

No, the real foundations of BMW racing success are sound basic design and tip-top engineering, and this has been proved time and again by the immaculate condition in which they finish the most arduous events.

Gilera Four

Statistics can fool you. They show, for example, that Gilera's tally of three TTs, six world individual championships and five manufacturers' titles is far from a record. What those bare statistics conceal, however, is the utter invicibility of the Italian double-knocker fours in 500cc classic racing in the mid-1950s. That was the highly competitive golden era when every European factory worth a damn weighed in with the finest machines it could design and a star-studded riding team. Indeed, it was only Gilera's withdrawal from racing at the close of the 1957 season (along with Moto-Guzzi and others) that left the field wide open for MV Agusta to start their phenomenal run of success with basically similar machines.

Gilera got their first taste of invincibility in 1939, when Dorino Serafini won the Ulster Grand Prix (then the world's fastest road race) at 97·85mph (record lap, 100·03 mph) – and with it the European 500cc championship, which at that time was decided on the results of a single selected event.

Not only did the tremendous power and speed of Serafini's supercharged Gilera (especially on the seven-mile Clady straight) make nonsense of Freddie Frith's truly heroic efforts on the unblown works Norton single, but the blown BMW twins, which had been the first to vanquish Joe Craig's legendary Nortons, didn't even show up in Belfast. Their superstar Georg Meier and most of their machines were unfit following prangs at Saxtorp and Sachsenring in frantic efforts to catch Serafini in the Swedish and German GPs.

In engineering terms, Gilera's pre-war dominance was inevitable. For supercharging gives an obvious power advantage over atmospheric induction. And, while a twin of the same total capacity has greater potential than a single, a four is even better than a twin.

Born as the Rondine in 1934, the original Gilera prototype had the 52×58mm water-cooled engine inclined forward at 40 degrees in a pressed-steel frame and supercharged by a meshing pair of three-lobe rotors. It

Cheeks flattened by the wind, Dorino Serafini rides his supercharged Gilera four to victory in the 1939 Ulster Grand Prix, so winning the European 500cc championship

produced 60bhp at 8,500rpm, when it won its first race, the 1935 Tripoli GP, where Piero Taruffi beat the formidable 120-degree Moto-Guzzi vee-twins. Immediately, the pressed-steel frame was ditched in favour of a duplex tubular one, with friction-damped rear springing, and Taruffi scooped the next race, too, the Pescara GP.

At the end of the year the makers (CNA, in Rome) sold the design to Gilera, and Taruffi embarked on an ambitious programme of record bids. Enclosing the machine in a beautifully fashioned shell boosted its speed by 35mph, though a tail fin had to be added to cure hairy handling from 155mph upward, and that made the bike susceptible to cross winds.

In the autumn of 1937, however, Taruffi clobbered Ernst Henne's BMW world 500cc record with 170·37mph, which marginally bettered Eric Fernihough's 1000cc record on the Brough Superior, too. Six months later the Italian added no fewer than seven miles to Jimmy Guthrie's hour record of 114 miles, set on a Norton.

Then, in the spring of 1939, Taruffi scored his most spectacular success. Riding back and forth along a 28-mile stretch of auto-strada between Brescia and Bergamo, he

tucked nearly 127 miles into an hour, in spite of having to stop and be humped round at each end, and coasting two miles to the fourth turn with a dry tank.

By then, Henne had snatched back the 500cc flying-kilometre record. But Serafini's resounding wins in Sweden, Germany and Ireland clearly showed which bike was top dog in the prestige sphere of road racing.

With supercharging banned after the war, Ing Pietro Remor recast the engine in a mould that set the pattern for all subsequent successful ohc fours. Air cooling was adopted and the engine stood more upright. There were four carburettors, separate cylinder barrels, two heads and full-width cam covers. To get a central ignition point with two valves, the plugs were recessed, firing the charge through narrow slots in the middle of the heads. Both the primary and camshaft drives were taken from the middle of the crankshaft and the integral gearbox had five speeds.

Soon the machines had the legs of the works Norton singles and Umberto Masetti won the world 500cc championship in 1950 and 1952. But Gilera speed and acceleration were frequently trumped by impeccable Norton handling and the supreme virtuosity

Top dog in pre-war road racing, Serafini's machine had friction-damped rear springing and a pressed-steel front fork. The water-cooled engine was inclined forward 40 degrees

81

Opposite top *an early ohc
racing Norton*

Above *a vee-four
Matchless Silver Hawk*

Opposite lower *a 250cc
radial-valve Rudge*

of Geoff Duke, who took the title in 1951.

The Gilera breakthrough came in 1953, when Duke finally acknowledged the writing on the wall and threw in his lot with the Italians. Liaising brilliantly with Taruffi (then development engineer) to add other raceworthy qualities to the machine's immense power, he scooped a hat-trick of world titles – a run stopped only by a six-month suspension in 1956 for supporting a riders' strike at Assen.

After near misses in the Senior TTs of 1953 and 1954, Duke completely dominated the 1955 event, and came so close to the first 100-mph lap that it was initially announced that he had done it. Yet, for all Duke's brilliance, it was the dour Bob McIntyre who made Gilera's final year of racing their most glorious.

Shortly before the 1957 TT, Duke damaged a shoulder in an accident at Imola and recommended the supremely talented Scot to Commendatore Gilera. Warming up with

The 500cc engine that made TT history in 1957 with the first ton lap. Camshaft drive is central, as are the plugs

a convincing win in the Junior, in spite of riding a whole lap on three cylinders before stopping for a plug change, McIntyre then notched one of the most magnificent Senior victories in Island history.

Though the race was lengthened to a punishing eight laps to commemorate the TT's golden jubilee, and though the Gilera carried seven gallons of petrol, he cracked in no fewer than four ton laps (leaving the record at a dizzy 101·12mph) and never eased the pace until signalled to do so by Geoff Duke when the Scot had a whopping 2½ minutes in hand over John Surtees (MV Agusta).

The after-effect of a neck injury sustained a few weeks later at Assen forced Mac to pass up the world 500cc championship to his team-mate Libero Liberati. But in Gilera's record-shattering spree on Monza's banked oval late in the November, the Scot handsomely eclipsed the best efforts of the top Italian stars.

Going for the world hour records (among others), Gilera had added a third wheel to one of the racers for Albino Milani to push the sidecar record up to 116 miles. But when Milani's brother Alfredo stuck a mere half-mile on Ray Amm's four-year-old Norton record by cramming 134 miles into an hour, Commendatore Gilera was clearly dissatisfied.

Watching from the by-lines, he had seen Milani gun the four on the straights, only to cut the power slightly on the diabolically bumpy turns. Convinced that McIntyre could dwarf the Italian star's performance, the boss ordered a telephone call to be put

A ghosted drawing of the five-hundred in its 1956 form, with full frontal fairing

84

through to Glasgow. Two days later Bob flew out, got the local hospital to certify him fit and started practising in the evening mist.

After sorting out the special magnesium-alloy streamlining, the bumps (particularly vicious with the tyre pressures at 60psi for cool running), the suspension and an ignition failure, Bob got down to business – choosing the three-fifty rather than the more powerful five-hundred simply because he could jam the throttles wide open and give all his attention and strength to the inevitable wrestling match, without having to juggle the twistgrip, too.

With the grip's friction adjuster screwed in hard, the initial gear changes were anything but silky. But once top gear was notched the grip stayed hard against the stop to the end. On the two straights, the revs soared to 11000rpm (about 145mph), though centrifugal force on the bankings brought the engine speed down to 10400rpm.

After an hour of increasing boredom for the indefatigable Scot, the engine cut dead when the tank ran dry. But not before the time was up, with 141·37 miles logged. It was the first time the classic hour record had been substantially bettered by a three-fifty. And although Mike Hailwood subsequently restored the honour to a five-hundred with 144·83 miles on an MV Agusta four round the far smoother Daytona bowl, the Gilera record still stands in its class – and will forever remain a monument to an indomitable rider and a superb machine.

Showing the low-slung oil container, Geoff Duke sweeps round La Source hairpin while leading the 1956 Belgian Grand Prix

The Imola slide that brought Duke to grief in 1957 and led to Bob McIntyre's taking over as No. 1 rider

Following pages Excelsior Mechanical Marvel with bronze cylinder head

Below McIntyre at Governor's Bridge during the most famous of all Senior TTs – the eight-lap golden jubilee race in 1957. Four days earlier he had won the Junior event

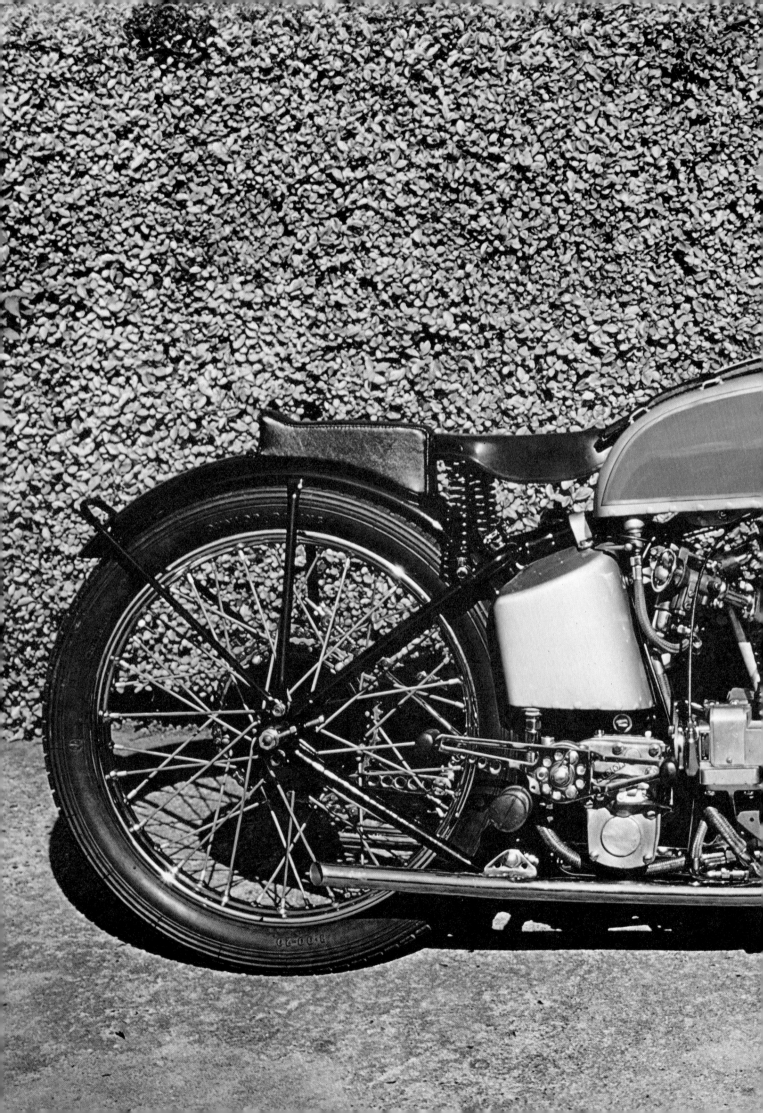

Brough Superior Dream

Should BMW ever want to narrow their transverse engines without sacrificing the perfect balance for which they are renowned, they could scarcely do better than copy the layout of the pre-war Brough Superior Dream and change from a flat twin to a flat four.

The Dream was no ordinary flat four, with a single crankshaft and one pair of cylinders behind the other. Instead, there were two crankshafts, one above the other and coupled by gears bolted on at the rear. Hence all four cylinders were equally exposed to the air for cooling and the engine was short as well as narrow (20in wide).

If the Dream was a brace of flat twins, they were flat twins with a difference. For each crankshaft had only one crankpin, to which both connecting rods (one forked, one plain) were attached. That way, the pistons did not move in and out in opposition to one another, but to the left and right together. Indeed, all four pistons moved left and right together. And, strange though it seems at first, that was the foundation of the engine's perfect balance. To understand that, one needs only an elementary grasp of engine balance; this is how it goes.

Consider a single cylinder. As the piston rushes upward it wants to keep on going but is restrained, and reversed by the connecting rod. At top dead centre, then, the piston exerts what is called a primary inertia force in an upward direction. And at bottom dead centre there is a similar downward force.

Clearly these vertical primary forces can be balanced completely by fitting heavy counterweights to the flywheels, diametrically opposite the crankpin, so that they act in opposition to the piston at both dead-

Sectioned drawing of the Brough Superior Dream engine in its revised form, showing the forked and plain connecting rods. The chain from the upper crankshaft drove the wet-sump oil pump, while the triangular chain drove the two camshafts

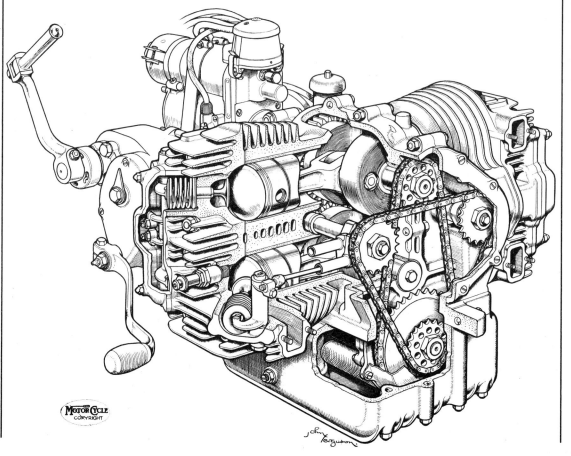

centre positions. Unfortunately, however, such counterweights exert unbalanced horizontal forces at the midstroke positions.

In practice, there is normally a compromise – balancing only part of the mass of the piston (and the upper portion of the con rod, which can also be regarded as reciprocating), leaving unbalanced forces of various degrees in various directions. The actual proportion balanced (called the balance factor) depends on the installation, for layouts vary in their resistance to forces in different directions.

So much for the primary forces. There are also secondaries (due to con rod angularity); these are only about a quarter as powerful as the primaries, but double the frequency – acting upward at both tdc and bdc, and downward every midstroke.

These principles can be applied to the Dream. When the pistons are all at the extreme left, the primary forces acting in that direction are cancelled by the massive flywheel bobweights pulling to the right, while the secondaries cancel out. And a similar happy situation applies when the pistons are all at the extreme right and the bobweights pulling to the left. But at midstroke there is no trouble from the bobweights, for the two sets are acting in opposite directions and cancel out. As for the secondary forces at midstroke, they are all acting inward, so cancel out, too.

For balance and cooling, then, the engine really was a dream. But George Brough's choice of name for his 1000cc flat four had a wider significance. Besides dynamo smoothness, it had unit construction of engine and gearbox, enclosed shaft drive, plunger-type rear springing and a special version of the Castle leading-link front fork. At that time these were all luxury features that set the machine on a pedestal – small wonder, for some very fertile brains were involved. Besides Brough the perfectionist, there was that great originator Freddie Dixon, and Ike Hatch (who was involved with such other unconventional layouts as the four-valve Excelsior Mechanical Marvel on which Sid Gleave won the 1933 Lightweight TT, the Francis-Barnett Stag, with crossover pushrods and straight rockers, and the triple-knocker AJS on which Rod Coleman won the 1954 Junior TT).

Fitting the flat-four engine into the general concept of the Dream was no great problem. The complete power unit was clamped at three points to the wide-spaced duplex loops of the welded frame. And the drive to the gearbox was taken from the lower crankshaft, through a two-plate cork clutch in a separate flywheel.

There was a choice of three or four speeds, the three-speed cluster having a normal kick-starter, the four-speed a hand lever with an

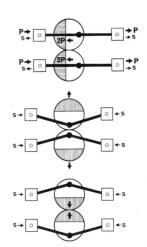

The sketch shows how the primary and secondary inertia forces are balanced not only at tdc and bdc but at midstroke, too

A rear view of the engine, showing the inlet ports, clutch arm and final-drive pick-up

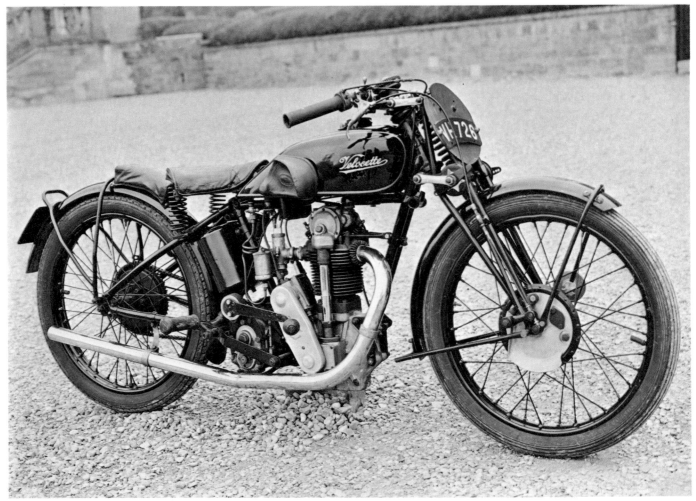

Opposite top *telescopic front fork version of the Triumph Speed Twin*

Opposite lower *a 350cc KTT Velocette from the early 1930s, with strutted front fork and George Dance kneegrips*

Above *in contrast with the other four machines on these pages, a 1975 BMW R90S*

Left *a reconditioned and modified ohc Velocette KTT*

anti-backfire release. As the gear cluster was so low, it was natural to use an underslung worm wheel, with enclosed shaft, for the final drive.

The original prototype engine had square bore-and-stroke dimensions (68 × 68mm) and the two camshafts were gear driven from the lower crankshaft. But many changes had been incorporated by the time the Dream made its début at the Earls Court Show in the autumn of 1938.

By then, bore and stroke were 71 × 63mm, with the domed pistons giving a compression ratio of 6·25:1 and having two compression rings above the gudgeon pin, one oil scraper below. More fundamentally, the camshafts were chain driven in a rather elaborate fashion.

From the front of the top crankshaft, a chain reached right down into the sump to drive the gear-type oil pump at half engine speed. Another sprocket on the front of the pump shaft drove a triangular chain that reached up again to the right and left camshafts, situated between the cylinder bores, with the exhaust lobes at the front, inlets at the rear.

To prevent the larger pump-shaft sprocket from churning and emulsifying the oil, it was enclosed in a pressed-steel shroud.

The tappets were long, with large bearing areas, so that the pushrods were short enough to be made of $\frac{3}{16}$in-diameter silver steel.

Split vertically down the middle, the crankcase incorporated the cylinder blocks, with centrifugally-cast iron liners. Bronze bushes were used for the main bearings, and the short, sturdy, light-alloy connecting

rods bore direct not only on the $\frac{5}{8}$in-diameter gudgeon pins but also on the $1\frac{3}{8}$in crankpins, which were formed integrally with the rear flywheel discs.

Left and right cylinder heads were cast in one piece, each served by its own Amal carburettor with butterfly throttle. Since the pistons moved in step, the 'sucks' on the carburettors were evenly spaced. The exhaust valves were in high-duty KE965 steel, the appreciably larger inlets in KE805.

Driven from the upper crankshaft, the Magdyno and distributor were mounted on a platform atop the gearbox. Light-alloy castings were used for not only the valve covers and inlet manifolds, but also for the primary exhaust manifolds, connected to the long chromium pipes.

Lubrication was very thorough. From the bolted-on sump, oil was drawn through a gauze and pressure-fed via a Tecalemit filter to the main, big-end and camshaft bearings, with a separate feed going out to the hollow rocker spindles. Return was by gravity.

As with a BMW, the transverse engine layout made for above-average accessibility for maintenance. And the rest of the bike matched up to the excellence of the engine. The rear wheel, with 9in-diameter drum brake, was quickly detachable. A well stocked tool box was concealed beneath the $4\frac{1}{2}$-gallon tank.

All of 18in wide, the luxurious saddle had a 2in backrest. And for the sidecar fan there was even a triangulated chassis, with two-point attachment and torsion-bar springing. Truly, the war put paid to an example of superb engineering.

Velocette Roarer

For British racing prestige in general, and for Velocette in particular, the outbreak of war in September 1939 was a profound technical tragedy. Though the factory raced on a shoestring, they had just had the courage and confidence to take up the massive Continental challenge with the most enterprising machine ever conceived in Britain. The tragedy was that it never fired in anger.

Along with Georg Meier's supercharged BMW twin and Dorino Serafini's blown Gilera four – whose sheer power and speed had finally outweighed the superior handling of the unblown British singles – the new Velo stood idle while the bombs fell, and was then outlawed for classic racing by the post-war ban on supercharging.

Nicknamed the Roarer, Velo's answer to the Continental challenge was a blown 500cc geared-crank parallel twin with shaft drive. Designed during the winter of 1938–39 and built in the following spring, it was put through its road paces in TT practising, then intensively developed for power. With a whole winter ahead for further development, and the brilliant Stanley Woods eager to go, the Roarer held out the rosiest prospects of restoring British supremacy in 1940. (At least the bike's architect, race-chief Harold Willis, was spared any frustration; tragically, he died of meningitis in June 1939.)

Bypassing the complexity of four cylinders, the Roarer incorporated the BMW's best points (superb engine balance and enclosed shaft drive) while avoiding its worst (vulnerability of the cylinder heads and a tendency to yaw on bad bumps). Strange as it may seem, the whole design hinged around the

Straddling the Velocette Roarer in the Isle of Man in 1939 is the great Stanley Woods. Behind him are spannerman Tommy Mutton (left) and Jim Owen, and (in white coat) development engineer Charles Udall

Following pages a rear-sprung DKW blown split single

93

rear tyre. Willis, having conceded that supercharging was essential to success, reasoned it was no use giving the rider the extra power unless the rear tyre was kept free from the drive-side oil film it often acquired from exposed chains.

So he settled for enclosed shaft drive, with a fore-and-aft crankshaft, as on the BMW. But the BMW's relative skittishness (compared with the British singles) was held to be due to its crankshaft disposition. Willis refused to join the chorus blaming torque reaction, arguing that so long as the drive was not interrupted, the only torque reaction was the one tending to loop the machine backward about the rear-wheel spindle, as with a transverse crankshaft and chain drive.

Instead, he identified the cause as gyroscopic precession of the crankshaft. This is nothing like so mysterious as it sounds. If you hold a pushbike wheel by the spindle ends, get someone to spin it, then tilt the spindle sharply in a vertical plane, you will find it precesses very strongly in a horizontal plane. Considering the weight and high revs of the BMW crankshaft and flywheel clutch, Willis calculated that its horizontal precession on bumps was strong enough to cause yawing.

Whatever the technical niceties, his solution was to neutralise all the forces by using two contra-rotating crankshafts geared together. The offset of the left shaft was convenient for the transmission, leaving the other to drive the supercharger and magneto. The considerable difference in height between the low-slung crankshafts and the final-drive shaft was spanned by using input and output gears of extra-large diameter in the integral, four-speed, all-indirect box.

With the cylinders stood side by side, the problem of vulnerability didn't arise – and well-nigh perfect balance was possible. By using a 100-per-cent balance factor (that is, counterweighting all the reciprocating mass

as well as the rotating mass), the vertical primary inertia forces were neutralised at top and bottom dead centres, and the unwanted horizontal forces arising from the bobweights at mid-stroke cancelled one another out within the crankcase. True, the alternating horizontal forces loaded the crankcase, but it was amply stiffened, and the ball and roller main bearings were massive.

From the six-vane Centric blower a long induction pipe swept up over the cylinder heads and divided to feed the forward-facing inlet ports. This arrangement was preferred to rear-facing inlets and a much shorter tract, because the extra capacity of the longer tract helped damp out pulsations, while its easier curves offered less resistance to gas flow.

It did involve rear-facing exhausts, and when liquid cooling was ditched for direct air cooling, scoops were fitted to deflect air on to the exhaust ports. But the straight pipes probably gave a power bonus. For a test-bench experiment with a 350cc KTT engine had shown that a straight exhaust system gave an extra $1\frac{1}{2}$bhp over the standard set-up.

Except that the pistons had a fourth ring apiece to help dissipate the extra heat, and the con rods had no sleeves in the big-end eyes (to cut engine width), detail design followed KTT practice pretty closely. The valves were opened by rockers from single camshafts, and these were driven by bevel gears and a vertical shaft between the cylinders.

As on the KTT, lubrication of all the vital parts – including the big ends, cams, bevels and coupling gears – was by calibrated jets. Magnesium alloy was used extensively throughout the machine. Even so, it weighed 370lb.

When Stanley Woods tried out the Roarer

With the cranks coupled by gears, the pistons rose and fell together. At tdc and bdc, their inertia forces were balanced by the massive bobweights, which opposed one another at midstroke

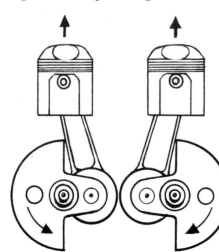
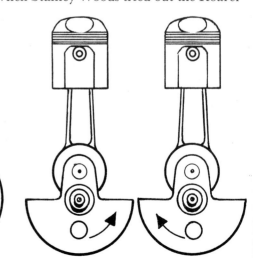

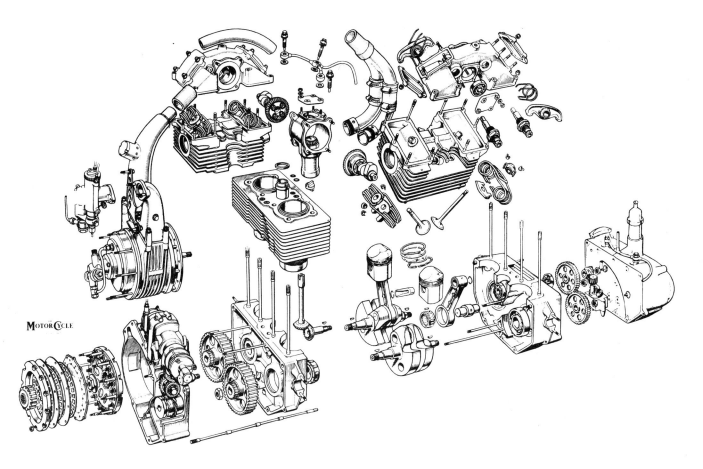

in TT practice, he found the theories on handling and engine balance amply vindicated. It steered to a hair and ran like a Rolls-Royce. And although the engine at that stage gave no more power than the unblown 500cc single, the smoother contours of the crankcase (with the rounded one-gallon oil tank bolted to the front) boosted top speed by 6mph to 130mph.

As always, the factory's power claim seemed very conservative compared with others. They never owned to more than 38bhp for the single, although it was just about as fast as the Norton, for which 50bhp was claimed.

According to Willis' carefully cultivated grapevine, Serafini's Gilera got its top whack of 140mph from no more than 50bhp. So the Roarer was geared to do 145mph at 7000rpm in top (3·737:1) – and the problem was then to find enough Hall Green horse-power to hit the target.

Already the engine spread its useful power range all the way from 2000rpm to 7000rpm, compared with 4500–6700rpm for the single. Back at the factory after the TT Charles Udall, assistant to Willis before the latter's death, started the search for more power.

By driving the blower separately from the engine, so that its relative speed could be varied, boost pressure was stepped up progressively from 4 to 13psi, while compression ratio was lowered from 8·75:1 to 7·5:1. Carburettor size was increased from $\frac{15}{16}$ in to $1\frac{1}{16}$ in and the valve timing was stretched. Within two months the engine was giving 54bhp net (62bhp at the gearbox, less eight to drive the supercharger), and the factory had every confidence of reaching, or even exceeding, target speed.

Had Europe continued to race motor cycles in 1940, instead of throwing bombs, it's a fair bet the opposition would scarcely have seen which way the Roarer went.

The left crankshaft drove the clutch, the right-hand one the supercharger, which fed forward-facing inlet ports. Camshaft drive was central, and the oil container was bolted to the front of the crankcase

97

DKW blown two-stroke

'The Dekkavay was a two-stroke and therefore a little more noisy, as you all knew before – and a little more faster, as you know now! Perhaps it could be improved, however, for next year's visit.' The fractured English of Herr Meurer, pre-war DKW race chief, embroidered his unexpected sense of humour. The occasion was the open-air prizegiving following Ewald Kluge's record-splintering victory in the 1938 Lightweight (250cc) TT. Meurer's succinct summing-up not only reflected the vast speed superiority of the 30-bhp Deek (with piston-type supercharger) but also hinted at the substantial power boost soon to come with an eccentric-vane compressor.

As to noise, the DKW's exhaust was not so much ear-splitting as soul-shattering. Kluge's full-bore descent of Bray Hill was said to have been heard on the Lancashire coast! Today's higher-revving unblown two-strokes are hard enough on the eardrums. By comparison, the Deek was well-nigh paralysing.

As with the BMW and Gilera four-strokes in the 500cc class, pre-war success came to to the smaller DKW two-strokes largely through the exploitation of supercharging at engine speeds which were low compared with those of today's unblown racers. In those days, most race engineers saw the symmetrical timing of piston-controlled ports – with the inevitably short inlet period and late exhaust closure – as an insuperable barrier to efficient breathing. DKW alone preserved an abiding faith in the two-stroke's racing potential.

Right from their track debut in 1925 with 175cc and 250cc machines, they used supercharging to offset the brevity of the inlet phase. Giving a modest 60bhp/litre, those first engines underlined the serious

On his record lap in the 1936 Lightweight TT, Stanley Woods screams his ear-splitting DKW split single down Bray Hill. The supercharger breathed through a reed valve

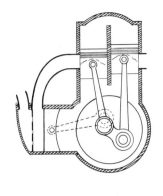
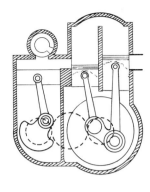
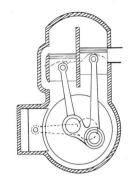
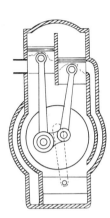
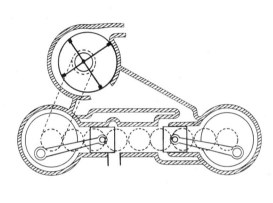
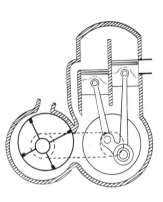

limitations imposed by symmetrical port timing in an era when inlet and exhaust resonances were nothing like so effectively harnessed as they have been since blowing was banned.

The bottleneck was eventually bypassed in 1931, when DKW got away from symmetrical timing by adopting the split-single layout. In this there were two cylinder bores, one behind the other in a single casting, with a common combustion chamber. The exhaust ports were in the rear bore, the transfers in the front.

Instead of the connecting rods being independent, as in a narrow-angle vee-twin such as the Matchless Silver Arrow, they were articulated. While the exhaust piston was connected to the main rod, the transfer piston was on a smaller rod, hinged to a boss on the front of the main big-end eye.

As a result, the exhaust piston had a permanent lead over the transfer piston, so that the exhaust ports not only opened before the transfers on the downstroke but closed before them on the upstroke, hence permitting more complete cylinder filling.

In the first DKW split single (a two-fifty) the supercharger was a large-diameter, short-stroke piston, working in a horizontal bore in the front of the crankcase and actuated by a separate connecting rod. As this piston moved inward, it breathed through two carburettors and an automatic reed valve. On the outward stroke it closed the reed valve and pumped the charge to the transfer ports.

Sure enough, peak power went up with a bang – and so did noise when exhaust megaphones were adopted in 1935! On his Isle of Man debut that year Arthur Geiss was seventh in the Lightweight TT. The following year he improved to third – and the team's number-one rider, Stanley Woods, broke the lap record, only to go out with a sick engine when leading on the seventh and final lap. Clearly the split single was on its way.

In 1937 there was another TT third place – by Ernie Thomas – after Ewald Kluge, making *his* IoM debut, had led in the early stages. But peak power stuck at 25bhp at 4000–4700rpm, for all attempts to push the

engine speed higher resulted in broken reeds.

So the reed valve was abandoned in favour of a cylindrical rotary valve, fed by a side-facing carburettor at each end. At the same time, the charging cylinder was switched from horizontal to vertical, its con rod actuated by a separate crank geared to the main crankshaft. An extension of the gear train went up to the rotor.

Introduced in 1936, this engine was developed for two years, by which time it gave 30 bhp at 6000—7000 rpm, before it was considered ripe for the TT. Handsomely smashing both lap and race records, Kluge led throughout, to become the first German to win a TT. What if his machine drank 12 gallons of fuel in the 264 miles? In spite of his five-gallon fuel load and extra pit stop, he finished with more than 11 minutes in hand.

Kluge used a similar engine when finishing second to Ted Mellors' double-ohc Benelli the following year (1939), when the eccentric-vane compressor Herr Meurer had hinted at in his Villa Marina speech was already under development. Chain driven from the crankshaft, the blower fed the crankcase, which thus served as a pressure-balance chamber, too. And it was just as well for the opposition that the war then interrupted classic racing – for the two-fifty's power took a tremendous leap from 30 bhp to 40 bhp, and a three-fifty was built on similar lines. . . .

During the five years between the end of the war and Germany's readmission to classic racing in 1951, the engine was developed a stage further (for national racing) by conversion to the opposed-piston principle, with the two pistons working crown-to-crown in opposite ends of a long cylinder. The two crankshafts were connected by a train of gears and it was a simple matter to give the exhaust piston any desired lead over the transfer piston.

In effect, this engine was a split single with the two cylinder bores swung out to opposite sides of the combustion chamber, and the compressor feeding a pressure-balance box surrounding the transfer ports. There were clear advantages in cylinder filling but the engine was unwieldy in shape.

Ingenious as they were, these grand prix layouts were by no means DKW's only variations on the supercharging theme. In a highly successful over-the-counter racer using crankcase induction, the horizontal charging piston was used in a different way. By moving forward as the exhaust and transfer pistons moved upward, it increased the engine's displacement far beyond the nominal 250cc. On the inward stroke, of course, crankcase compression was similarly boosted. In this case it was the back, not the front, of the large piston crown that did the supercharging.

An earlier variant on this principle (made in several sizes) had the charging piston in the bottom, not the front, of the crankcase. But that made the shape of the crank chamber much less compact and the engine too tall.

It seems a pity that all this ingenuity eventually came to nought with the post-war ban on blowing. But supercharging clearly made nonsense of the capacity formula, and the only legitimate method left is the so-called free supercharging obtained by harnessing the gas resonances, which has been the main theme of two-stroke development since the war.

Velocette Mk VIII KTT

The scene around the Velocette stand at the Earls Court Show in 1938 was reminiscent of London's January sales and the hordes of bargain-hunting women fighting to get at the goods. But the hordes were not women, of course, they were road-racing motor cyclists.

The star attraction, priced at £120, was that last and most famous of the long line of KTT racers, the Mark VIII. With the massive finning on its light-alloy cylinder and head, its 11-to-1 compression ratio, multi-jet oiling, Dowty oleo-pneumatic pivoted-fork rear springing, magnesium-alloy cone hubs and telescopic guide for the front-fork spring, it was virtually a catalogue

version of the works bike on which Stanley Woods, backed up by Ted Mellors, had comfortably broken Norton's seven-year monopoly of the Junior TT only five months earlier, relegating even the brilliant Freddie Frith to third place.

The Mark VIII was, in fact, the nearest thing to a works special that had been marketed since production of the preceding KTT had been stopped three years earlier. In the interval, Velocette design and development had been in a state of flux. In 1935 the Mark V KTT already had the jet oiling system, the cylinder and head clamped to the crankcase by the same long bolts, and

Best of all the KTT Velocettes – the Mark VIII. Wheel rims were in high-tensile steel, cone hubs in magnesium alloy. The mudguard pad was air-filled and the rear springing oleo-pneumatic

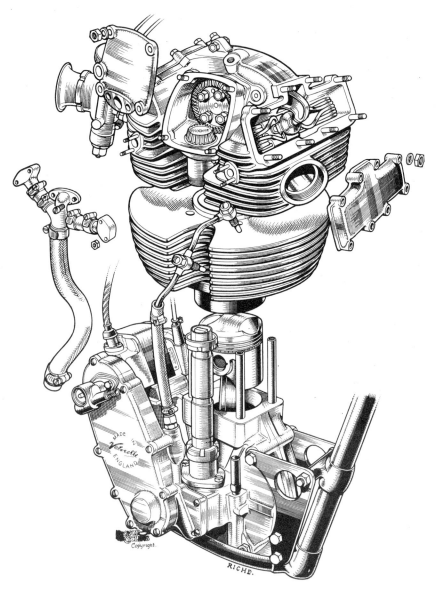

the gearbox bolted top and bottom between the rear engine plates instead of suspended from a frame lug. But it retained the iron cylinder and aluminium-bronze head.

For 1936, two different racing engines were tried. One was virtually a Mark V KTT with double camshafts driven from the upper bevel shaft by a five-gear train, and only the valves and hairpin springs exposed. Development engineer Harold Willis dropped this like a hot brick when the fracture of an Oldham coupling was traced directly to the revised camshaft layout.

The other engine had a single camshaft, the cambox cast integrally with the aluminium-alloy cylinder head and the valve gear fully enclosed – as on the KSS roadster of the same year. This was the only Mark VI KTT made and it was ridden by Austin Munks to win the Junior Manx Grand Prix in the September.

But in the June, the pivoted-fork rear suspension, with air springing and oil damping, had made its début in the TT, along with the telescopic guide for the front-fork spring, to relieve it of bending stresses.

The distinctive 9in-square cylinder-head finning was introduced on the works racers in 1937. And when a similar-looking engine was installed in an unsprung cradle frame and catalogued as the Mark VII KTT the following spring (1938), with a compression ratio of 8·75 to 1 and plain steel hubs, the production run of about 25 was quickly snapped up.

Indeed, when details of the 1939 range

Above this engine has the 8·75-to-1 piston standardised on the Mark VII and resurrected for Pool petrol in the Mark VIII after the war. Note the oiling jets for the upper bevel gears and cams

Right on the works model, of which the Mark VIII was a replica, Stanley Woods wins the 1939 Junior TT for the second year running

In the 1949 Swiss Grand Prix, world 350cc champion Freddie Frith holds off the AJS challenge of Les Graham (No. 4) and Bill Doran

The author on the Brooklands Mountain circuit in 1939. Note the obligatory silencer. At that meeting he gained the only 350cc Gold Star to be won on petrol, not alcohol fuel

were released in September 1938, it was still the Mark VII that was listed for the racing man. The speed with which it was ousted by the rear-sprung Mark VIII in time for the Earls Court Show – despite the factory's pre-occupation with the then-secret blown 500cc Roarer (page 93) – was eloquent of Velocette enterprise at that time.

That the resounding success of the works Velo in the 1938 Junior TT was no flash in the pan was emphasised when Stanley Woods repeated his win in 1939 (the day after Harold Willis tragically died of meningitis). The majority of the other finishers were on private Velos, too.

So advanced was the design for its time that it also won the first three post-war Juniors and the first two world 350cc championships (Freddie Frith 1949, Bob Foster 1950) before Joe Craig's works Nortons got the upper hand. While Frith and Foster occasionally used twin-camshaft engines, they generally preferred the more tractable single knocker.

Private owners, too, had a ball with the Mark VIII. My own 1939 model was the only three-fifty ever to win a Brooklands Gold Star (for lapping at 100mph) without using alcohol fuel. This was particularly satisfying because the engine's high performance relied heavily on the megaphone exhaust whereas, at Brooklands, a 'silencer' to specified dimensions was obligatory.

Coveting a Gold Star, I had substituted a foot of plain piping for the megaphone and stuck the so-called Brooklands can on the

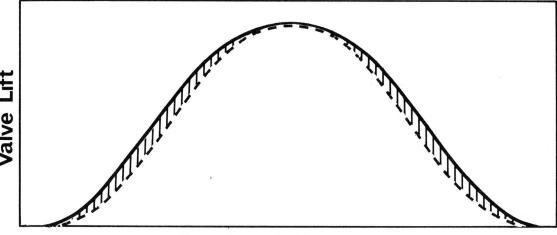

Valve Lift

Crankshaft Degrees

Valve motion with the larger rocker-heel radius (solid line) compared with standard (broken line). The shaded area represents deeper breathing, while the shorter initial acceleration period cures valve float

end. The idea was that, if the Mark VIII, thus detuned, would lap at 97mph or so on petrol, it might be worthwhile having a special piston made, to boost compression to about 15:1, to try for a Gold Star on methanol.

To my great delight, the experiment, in a 10-lap race, produced a lap speed of 102·06 mph, and the expense of a special piston was obviated. But not, to my sorrow, the much heavier expense of an engine rebuild. For close on 30 miles of full throttle in top gear had overstressed the KE965 exhaust valve, which objected by dropping into the cylinder at full speed on the very next outing, at Donington. No wonder the works bikes had sodium-cooled valves!

As with the professionals, we privateers wheeled out our old Mark VIIIs after the war and began to win races. We also developed the bikes according to our lights. And an ankle-deep pile of swarf in my workshop one winter testified to a weight saving of some 50lb (from the original 320lb) by making as many parts as possible (even including spoke nipples) in aluminium alloy.

The snag to that little escapade was that, since most of the weight saving was on sprung parts, the all-important ratio of sprung to unsprung mass was lowered, and the standard springing was then much too hard.

That was not the only problem with the springing. The air capacity of the Dowty rear struts was so small that even the swiftest application of a pressure gauge to the Schrader valves (standard pressure 35psi) released 2 to 3psi. Moreover the seals were not always up to their job – and loss of air and oil during a race could make the bike a pig to handle.

Regrettably, some of the post-war Mark VIIIs, though supposedly identical, were inferior in workmanship and performance to

the pre-war ones. My own 1950 model was 12mph down on speed and poorly machined, while the valves floated, to the severe detriment of the cam closing flanks, some 600rpm short of the claimed peak-power revs of 7000rpm!

This led me to try a larger radius on the rocker heels ($\frac{5}{8}$in instead of the standard $\frac{13}{32}$ in), which not only cured the trouble but permitted the rocker-return springs to be dispensed with and gave a power boost into the bargain. My sketch explains both effects.

First, the larger radius gave much fiercer initial acceleration to the valves, so starting their deceleration sooner and giving the springs that much longer to slow and reverse their motion. That put an end to the valve float. Second, the greater area under the valve-lift curve represents deeper breathing and better scavenging, hence more power.

Later on, the factory went part way along this road by increasing the cam-follower radius to $\frac{1}{2}$in. But not before they had tried the ill-starred expedient of chromium plating the cams instead – ill-starred because flakes of plating were known to break off and jam the oil pump.

Another contribution to the post-war deficiency in performance was an old-fashioned flattening of the inlet port. This was done to leave more metal in its roof, so that port enlargement didn't break through into the valve-spring well. Recutting the port to the pre-war shape gave an unmistakable improvement.

But these post-war problems detracted not one whit from the brilliance of the original design. So far as production models were concerned, the Mark VIII KTT typified the initiative, superb engineering and soundly-based confidence that put Velocette on the map in their golden years; without it they subsequently slipped off.

AJS Porcupine

Despite Les Graham's world 500cc championship in 1949, and some spectacular performances in that and other years, the AJS Porcupine double-knocker twin goes down in history as the design that was caught on the hop. For it was laid out during the Second World War specifically as a supercharged design, and time was too short to recast it when blowing was banned just before classic racing restarted. So long as it was raced, the Porcupine was handicapped by the enforced switch to atmospheric induction.

During the war there was precious little leisure time for anyone, but such as the AJS boffins had they whiled away planning their post-war challenger. Remembering the clear mastery that supercharging had given the BMW and Gilera five-hundreds in the late 1930s, and inspired by the example of the Velocette Roarer (page 93), they never considered anything but a blown engine.

That is why a supercharger cradle was formed on top of the integral four-speed gearbox. It is also why the cylinders were prone – to make the most of direct air cooling for the heads. For getting surplus heat away from the combustion chambers was a paramount aim – and the spike head finning that gave the machine its nickname, though vulnerable and difficult to cast, was reckoned the most effective for a given depth and pitch.

As soon as the war was over, rough plans were translated into detailed design and a prototype was made. Then came the shock of the blower ban – and all that could be done at that late stage was to make a fresh cylinder head giving an appreciably higher compression ratio.

Though a step in the right direction, this was only a partial solution to the problem. For the long, curved induction tracts, deliberately chosen for their volume before

Here leading the 1949 Senior TT, the ever-popular Les Graham had victory snatched away when the magneto shaft sheared two miles from the finish

World 500cc champion Les Graham after his Swiss Grand Prix win in 1950. In shirtsleeves is development engineer Matt Wright

Opposite top the AJS 500cc racing twin got its nickname 'Porcupine' from the spike finning of the cylinder head

Opposite bottom the 1951 tank shape emphasises the space above the gearbox, where the supercharger was to have been in the original concept

the ban, proved to be a major headache. Clean low-speed carburation was extraordinarily elusive, and many inlet-pipe layouts were tried in an attempt to take the tantrums out of acceleration.

Painstaking development work eventually pushed up the peak power from 40 bhp in 1947 – when Ted Frend scored a great win in the Dunholme 100-mile Grand Prix – to 55 bhp in the mid-1950s. But even at that level the engine was sadly under-developed. At all stages, it gave its best power at 7600 rpm, whereas with its $68 \times 68 \cdot 5$ mm bore and stroke it should have peaked at no less than 9000 rpm and given at least 60 bhp. Clearly, the cam forms chosen for comparatively low engine speeds and high boost pressures

seriously inhibited the engine's unblown performance.

Handling was another problem. Though the original cylinder layout kept the centre of gravity fairly low, and though a great deal of thought went into the design of the wide duplex-loop frame – which was welded from oval-section as well as round tubing – the damping of the AJS suspension struts was inadequate, and factory policy forbade a change to proprietary units.

All the same, the Porcupine was sufficiently competitive early on to justify the dash of the riders. And in his championship year Les Graham came within an ace of what would undoubtedly have been one of the most popular Senior wins in TT history.

After taking the lead when Bob Foster's Moto-Guzzi vee-twin succumbed to clutch trouble, Graham was only two miles from the chequered flag when the magneto shaft sheared, leaving him to push home a gallant 10th.

From then on, the Porcupine's TT performances were consistent if not spectacular, with Graham fourth to the three works Nortons in 1950, Bill Doran second to Geoff Duke's Norton the following year, and Rod Coleman fourth in both 1952 and 1953.

As befits a blown design, engine construction was very robust. A one-piece forging, the backward-rotating crankshaft was supported in a 1¾in-bore double-flanged plain bearing in the middle and a roller bearing at each end. The crankcase-gearcase and bolted-on sump were cast in Elektron (magnesium alloy), while the shell-bearing connecting rods were forged in RR56 aluminium alloy. Also forged, the pistons had full skirts.

Though the liberally finned and deeply spigoted light-alloy cylinders were separate, there was a one-piece cylinder head incorporating wells for the overlapping hairpin valve springs. Sodium cooling was used for the exhaust valves. Drive to the camshafts was by a train of eight gears running on roller bearings, with an outrigger plate supporting the ends of the spindles. The camshafts were hollow forgings, and each was supported in five 1in-diameter roller bearings, clamped in Elektron boxes. An additional gear took the drive from the ohc train to the oil pump and magneto atop the crankcase.

Oil circulation was at the rate of 45 gallons an hour at 7000rpm, and the main feeds were to the middle main bearing and the cam boxes. A bleed off the scavenge line from the sump to the 1½-gallon oil tank lubricated the rear chain via drillings in the sprocket.

A pair of spur gears ⅝in wide took care of the primary drive. In view of the high torque expected from a blown engine the ventilated clutch was run fast – about 0·7 times engine speed. Roller bearings were used in the gearbox, for the free pinions as well as the shafts, and the final drive was on the opposite side to the primary.

Developments over the years included canting the cylinders up 45 degrees and changing to normal finning; one-gallon sump oiling; many frame and tank alterations; and chain drive for the magneto, which finally put an end to shaft fracture. The FIM ban on blowing was very logical, but it was a great pity that it prevented the true paces of the Porcupine being shown.

Benelli single

Throughout the history of European road racing, the high-revving lightweight single has been as typically Italian as Chianti or pizza. So when, in the decade before the Second World War, there was a wholesale rush to supercharged multis as the easiest road to power, it was hardly surprising that the hero of the rearguard action was the bright-red Italian 250cc double-knocker Benelli, for none of the British lightweights – Excelsior, Rudge, New Imperial – could muster anything like the speed to challenge the DKW blown two-stroke.

The Benelli's greatest pre-war achievement was gained in the 1939 Lightweight TT, when Ted Mellors beat the previous year's winner, Ewald Kluge (blown DKW), by no less than 3 minutes 45 seconds. Although he had notched up wins galore on the Continent, it had long been Mellors' top ambition to win a TT. It was at Monza the previous September that he became

In vile weather, Ted Mellors squelches to an emphatic victory in the 1939 Lightweight TT. The 250cc Benelli was faster than many works three-fifties

convinced the Benelli would give him the best chance of doing that. For there Soprani had won the 250cc class of the 1938 Italian Grand Prix, with higher lap and race speeds than the records Mellors himself set in winning the 350cc race on his Velocette.

Based on a 1933 design, the Benelli had its camshafts driven by a long train of gears, which also served the magneto and oil pump. There was an external flywheel in a case on the left, with an outrigger bearing, and the oil was contained in a ribbed compartment cast on the bottom of the small crankcase. Lubrication was very thorough, and circulation rate so high that an oil cooler was necessary. As usual on Italian engines, the crankcase breather had a very large bore. And a clue to the engine's high-speed breathing ability was the carburettor choke size of $1\frac{5}{32}$ in, uncommonly large for its day.

Left *after his TT win, Mellors is surrounded by the delighted Italian team in the winner's enclosure*

Below *a much-modified 250cc Benelli racer spotted in the Silverstone paddock in the spring of 1962*

on an old practice hack. Next day he shook the DKW camp by lapping within two seconds of Kluge's 1938 record. When the pukka race bike arrived, it cheekily showed its megaphone to the best Juniors, despite their extra 100cc. And the red Italian flyer was so reliable that the only maintenance called for in the Island was a change of jet size.

Since Mellors weighed 170lb – uncommonly heavy for a pre-war 250cc jockey – there was clearly no exaggeration in the makers' claim of 30bhp. On the level the engine revved eagerly to 8400rpm (little short of 110mph on the 5·75:1 top gear); downhill it romped to 9000rpm (115mph). Below 6000rpm the power faded rapidly; above that speed it came in with a rush. Consequently, the clutch and gears came in for plenty of use – and the pre-race warming-up drill was unusually long, to get the oil thin enough for the wet clutch plates to free fully.

During the race, the weather deteriorated from poor to vile, but Mellors anticipated it and took the precaution of cross-cutting the treads of both 2·75in-section tyres to improve wet grip. By the Gooseneck in the first lap (25 miles) Omobono Tenni, on a blown Moto-Guzzi single, had wiped out Mellors' 30-second starting advantage. For a few miles Mellors took the bait. Then, confident the Moto-Guzzi would not last the seven laps, he let it go.

By the end of the lap Tenni led his teammate Stanley Woods by 8 seconds, with Mellors third, 37 seconds adrift. But Mellors' judgement in not attempting to match the Moto-Guzzis' cracking pace was soon vindicated. For Tenni slowed on the second lap, and Woods spent six minutes at his pit, so that Mellors led comfortably from Tenni, with Kluge moving into third spot on the Deek.

From then on Mellors was never headed, though some heartbeats were missed in the Benelli camp when he had to make three attempts to restart after his first pit stop. Tenni went out on lap three, Woods fought back fiendishly and climbed up to third before his engine died on lap five. But by then the gaps between the leading riders were much too wide for the issue to be decided by anything save mechanical reliability, and with the Benelli going like a train, while Kluge's plugs jibbed at the atrocious weather, the result was never in doubt.

Advanced as their single was, Benelli were anything but blind to the advantages of

Top note the oil cooler in the scavenge line

Above the outside flywheel was normally encased, not exposed as here

Although the front fork was of conventional girder pattern, the rear springing was a composite of pivoted-fork and plunger layouts, with friction damping. Dry weight was 275lb.

In the first morning's practice for the TT, Mellors comfortably headed the lightweights supercharging and multi-cylinders. When Moto-Guzzi got the bugs out of their blown single later in the year, Mellors looked forward to trouncing them in 1940 on one of the most enterprising lightweights ever – a blown four producing 52bhp at 10000rpm. Alas, the war intervened. But while the subsequent ban on supercharging made the new bike ineligible, it also gave the old single a new lease of life.

On it, the spectacular Dario Ambrosini made monkeys of some of the best three-fifties in 1949, though, on his first appearance in the TT that year, he squandered his chances by tumbling at the Nook on the first lap and damaging an arm too badly to continue. The following year he made no mistake. Slowed initially by the top hamper of an extra 2½ gallons of petrol in the seat fairing for a non-stop seven laps, he was a modest fifth at the end of the opening lap, a minute down on the leader, Maurice Cann (Moto-Guzzi).

But as the top hamper lessened, Ambrosini climbed inexorably through the massed-start field. Third on lap three, second two laps later, he was on Cann's tail on lap six. Then, with a final record lap at 80·91mph, he overhauled the Moto-Guzzi star to win by a mere five or six yards after nearly 3½ hours' racing. Sustaining his brilliant form throughout the season, he clinched both the individual and manufacturers' world 250cc championships for Benelli.

An unblown version of the four was rumoured for 1951 but it was, in fact, the old single on which Ambrosini turned out again. Still a lone hand, he continued to trounce the opposition and pile up points towards another world championship, though over-jetting in the hot TT cut his revs from 9600 rpm to 9100rpm, and Tommy Wood (Moto-Guzzi) beat him by 8·4 seconds. Alas, in practising for the French Grand Prix on the 5½-mile Albi circuit in the July, Ambrosini skidded on a patch of tar melted by the scorching sun and was killed instantly when he rammed a telegraph pole. The race, and the world championship, were then a gift to Bruno Ruffo (Moto-Guzzi), for Ambrosini *was* Benelli – and without him the challenge from the small Pesaro factory died, too.

With a record seventh and final lap, Dario Ambrosini (Benelli) snatches the 1950 Lightweight TT from Moto-Guzzi star Maurice Cann

Harley-Davidson

Like so many other machines of highly individual character, Harley-Davidson vee-twins have always evoked strongly contrasting feelings. Nothing can damp the factory's pride, or Harley enthusiasts' joy, that a Sportster engine, enlarged to 1480cc and fuelled with nitro-methane, powered the 19ft-long streamliner in which Cal Rayborn hurtled feet first to his phenomenal world speed record of 265·492mph at Bonneville in the Fall of 1970. Yet, east of the Atlantic, where riders have long been weaned on much smaller, lighter, handier machines, it is not difficult to find someone who regards the American heavyweights as almost agricultural by comparison.

History records that the Milwaukee concern was one of only two American motor-cycle manufacturers to survive the shattering impact of the mass-produced cheap car in the early 1920s (Indian was the other); also that H-D have stood alone since Indian eventually succumbed in 1962. What's more – notwithstanding the speed-cop image that lingers in Europe – Harley-Davidson have a long and enviable record of Stateside racing successes, even though there was a period when the rules were framed to handicap the most competitive of the European imports, notably the ohc Manx Nortons.

Not that H-D speed achievements were confined to America. Indeed, in the middle years of Britain's banked concrete bowl at Brooklands, two works 1000cc racers, with overhead inlet and side exhaust valves, were sent over in a bid to break the 100-mph

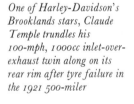

One of Harley-Davidson's Brooklands stars, Claude Temple trundles his 100-mph, 1000cc inlet-over-exhaust twin along on its rear rim after tyre failure in the 1921 500-miler

barrier. They were ridden by Claude Temple and Doug Davidson, and it was Davidson (no relative of the factory family) who first clocked a three-figure speed, with 100·76 mph in April 1921, beating Temple by a fifth of a second over a flying kilometre.

However, Temple soon recouped, with the first Brooklands 90-mph lap, the world five-mile record (twice in three months), then records for the classic hour, the flying kilo and flying mile, the last at exactly 100 mph – and all within five months.

The legendary and colourful Freddy Dixon, too, hit many a British headline on a big-twin Harley-Davidson, although his was the model with eight overhead valves and four exhaust pipes. Practically unbeatable in hill-climbs and sprints, he set a new high-water mark of 103·44 mph at the half-mile Clipstone Speed Trials in July 1924. Just over a year later he won the Brooklands 1000cc championship at 100·1 mph, using no exhaust pipes whatsoever. Then, a year later still, he lifted the world flying-kilometre

record to 106·8 mph at the Bois de Boulogne.

In the face of the inevitable British take-over in big-twin racing (by ohc Anzani and ohv JAP engines) Frank Longman kept the H-D flag flying a few years longer at Brooklands with an inlet-over-exhaust model, winning the very first Hutchinson 100, in May 1925, at 89·66 mph, and the 1000cc 200-miler three months later at 85·41 mph. But if the American big twins were doomed to bow to home-bred machinery in Britain, H-D singles managed to carry the factory's fame forward into the dirt-track era. In the early years of the sport (the late 1920s), when there were any number of competitive makes, the Harley Peashooter was one of the most formidable models, especially in the capable hands of American Sprouts Elder. Strangely enough, it was a lightweight development of the company's 350cc single-cylinder roadster.

Another little-known Harley-Davidson model was the 574cc flat-twin 5–35, the code deriving from 5hp and 35cu in. First

No exhaust pipes! Freddie Dixon at Brooklands on the 1000cc eight-valve Harley Davidson he often raced without pipes

marketed in 1913, it continued in production for a few years after the First World War. But although Bill Harley and Arthur Davidson established their commercial foothold, just after the turn of the century, with belt-driven, inlet-over-exhaust singles as raw as any machines at that time, it was not long before they switched to the vee-twin layout that has long been their real hallmark.

Engine capacities have ranged beyond 1300cc, but it was the choice of 750cc, in about 1929, along with the change from overhead-inlet to side-by-side valves (the so-called flat-head layout), that set the pattern for the future. It was a descendant of that original WL45 flat-head seventy-fifty that served the US Army throughout the Second World War. A few years after the war it was replaced by the same-size Model K with hydraulic front and rear suspension.

In 1954 the Model K was enlarged to 901cc, as the KH, which was superseded only a year later by the Sportster. But the Model K's greatest claim to fame was that it sired the famous KR racer, winner of so many American national championships.

Actually, Harley-Davidson first established a racing department way back in 1914, under the stimulus of a host of private successes. Starting by winning the Dodge City 300-miler (at that time America's top prestige event), they went from strength to strength, monopolising nationals, endurance runs, miniature TTs, road races and dirt-track championships, besides setting numerous records on Daytona Beach – using, first, the inlet-over-exhaust layout, then the eight-valver and finally a 1000cc ohv model.

After the Second World War, a new points system was introduced to decide the national championship, and Harley-Davidson dominated it from the start, as they did the Daytona Beach races and the Jack Pine Enduro. Joe Leonard was the first of a string of H-D champions, followed by such stars as Carroll Resweber, Bert Markel and Roger Reiman.

Then, when the steeply-banked, super-fast Daytona International Speedway was opened in 1961, Reiman scored the first of his many wins in the 200-mile championship race. But it was the brilliant Cal Rayborn who made history there, in 1968, by scoring the first ton-up win (at 101·29mph) and lapping the entire field in the process. Two years later Rayborn brought the factory its most spectacular success, when he pushed the world speed record beyond 265mph.

In that venture, Rayborn was much more than the supremely lonely and intrepid pilot who lay flat on his back in a 2ft-diameter aluminium tube as it roared, bucked and creaked down miles of marker line across the desolate salt flats. He was also responsible for sorting out the high-speed handling problems inseparable from such an unorthodox layout. In run after run, diagnosing and correcting faults, Rayborn took prangs in his stride. First when he inadvertently lowered the low-speed stabilising skids at 130mph, sending the streamliner tumbling end over end. Then when he elected not to use the skids at all the machine just toppled over at 50mph. Alas, Rayborn is dead – killed racing an unfamiliar 500cc Suzuki twin in New Zealand. But his fame lives on.

Above *Joe Petrali's 1937 American 1000cc record holder, with disc wheels and partial streamlining.*

Upper left *Cal Rayborn pops a parachute to slow from 265mph at Bonneville.*

Lower left *Rayborn shoe-horns himself into the 2ft-diameter projectile*

Vincent Big Twin

In spawning one of the greatest designs of all time – the Vincent big twin – a flash of sheer inspiration achieved more than any amount of premeditation. Sitting at his board in Stevenage one day in 1936 was Australian Phil Irving, as brainy an engineer as ever graced the motor-cycle industry; on the board were a drawing and a tracing – both of the timing-side crankcase half of the firm's 500cc high-camshaft single. Idly, Irving turned the tracing over on top of the drawing and lined up the centres of the crankshaft pinion and the idler wheel in the timing gear.

His brilliant intuition recognized a sudden possibility. 'Here, look at this,' he called to Phil Vincent, boss of the outfit. For there, clear as daylight, was a ready-made layout for the timing-side crankcase half of a 1000cc 47-degree vee-twin. It was an odd cylinder angle, to be sure, but it meant that the extra crankcase holes for the second cylinder could be produced simply by inverting the original drilling jig, just as Irving had inverted the tracing. For the idler gear of the five-hundred happened to be offset $23\frac{1}{2}$ degrees from the cylinder axis.

At that time, the high-camshaft single had been in production for only a year because Vincent – after buying his way into the industry by acquiring the defunct HRD concern – had initially been content to fit various proprietary makes of engine, while concentrating his own design activities on rear springing and dual brakes. But a bellyful of JAP engine troubles in the 1934 Senior TT had convinced him he must design his own engine, too.

Made in standard (Meteor), sports (Comet) and racing (TT Replica) guises, that engine was bang up to date, to say the least, and in many ways was advanced. The crankcase mouth was carried halfway up the five-stud cylinder barrel. The short, tapered pushrods were splayed at 62 degrees to lie parallel to the valves, which they opened through straight, transverse rockers. And each valve had two short guides, the rocker end being forked to bear on a valve-stem collar between them. Valve closure was by exposed double-hairpin springs at the top.

Soon, that drawing-board crankcase layout was translated into metal and two Meteor top halves were clamped on – the rear one offset to the right to assist cooling and obviate the need for a forked connecting rod. Fortunately, a suitable frame was handy – built with the top tube three inches longer than standard, to house a JAP engine for Eric Fernihough.

In production, the frame was lengthened

Series C version of the Vincent Rapide. Fork blades were light-alloy forgings controlled by long springs and a hydraulic strut. A similar strut damped the rear springing

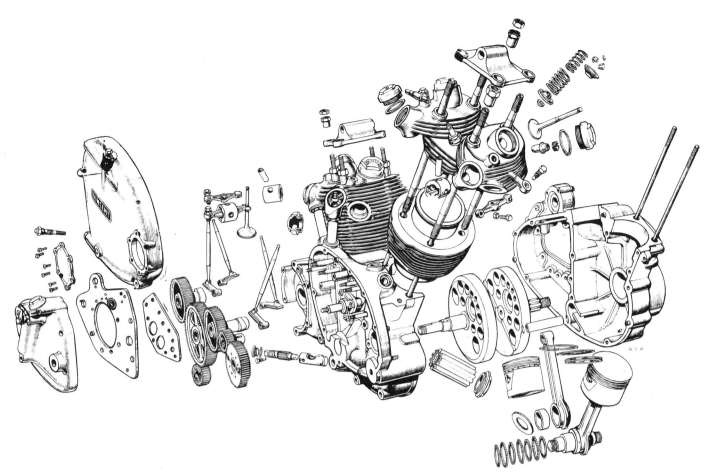

a further half inch (stretching the wheel-base to $58\frac{1}{2}$in). Even so, the springs for the front exhaust and rear inlet valves left precious little room for the enamel on the down tubes! And the only way to house the front carburettor was to specify a horizontal mixing chamber.

Affectionately dubbed the plumber's nightmare because of the maze of external oil pipes, the Series A Rapide (as the first twin was catalogued) set unprecedented standards in effortless high performance. Eloquent of its sheer versatility was an achievement by Jim Kentish, an early private customer.

After commuting one Saturday morning to the Kew Theatre, where he was stage manager, he took time off during the matinée to nip over to Brooklands. There he won a Gold Star for lapping at over 100mph, before trundling quietly back to the theatre in time for the evening performance. More seriously, George Brown (then an experimental tester at the factory) entered a Rapide for the *Motor Cycle* Clubman's Day at Brooklands, clocked nearly 113mph through the kilometre trap and lapped at just under 106mph.

However, the Burman four-speed transmission had never been designed for the massive torque of the Rapide. First weakness

brought to light by uninhibited use of the twistgrip was clutch slip. When that was cured, and the torque got through to the gearbox, the layshaft bearings failed. Modify those, and the casing split. . . .

No sooner had the Second World War run its course than Vincent and Irving came up with an answer that had connoisseurs and young bloods alike falling over themselves to place their orders. A complete redesign, the Series B Rapide did full justice to the complementary talents of the two Phils – Vincent imaginative and fanciful, Irving sound and practical.

As before, the theme was a Jekyll and Hyde sort of machine – a comfortable, mild-mannered roadburner capable, with a little tuning, of world-record performances. Just about all that remained of the pre-war specification were the 84×90mm bore and stroke, the pivoted-triangle rear springing and the duplex brakes.

To suit the available magnetos, the cylinder angle was increased to 50 degrees. The wheelbase was shortened by dispensing with a conventional frame and using the integral engine and gearbox as a structural member, suspended from a six-pint, box-section oil tank that doubled up as a top tube.

Both carburettors had vertical mixing chambers. Driven by a blade-tensioned

Series B Rapide engine, showing the three-row crowded-roller big ends. Each valve had two guides, and the forked rocker actuated a collar on the stem between them

triplex chain, the clutch had an ingenious self-servo action, in which engine torque forced a pair of pivoted shoes into contact with the drum. And the whole machine bristled with riders' points, such as the minutely adjustable riding position, instant chain setting without tools, and so on.

Inevitably, sporting (Black Shadow) and racing (Black Lightning) models followed, their cylinders and heads anodised black, the crankcase and covers stove-enamelled. On the Series C versions, the friction-damped Brampton front fork was superseded by the Girdraulic pattern, with forged light-alloy blades, two pairs of long, soft springs and a hydraulic damper. A similar damper took over from the friction bands in the rear springing.

Magnificent roadsters though the post-war twins were, their renown spread quickest

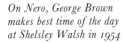

On Nero, George Brown makes best time of the day at Shelsley Walsh in 1954

Nero in sprint trim, with AMC telescopic front fork and brake, and a Velocette pivoted rear fork with proprietary struts

through their sporting successes. George Brown was the most persistent protagonist – terrorising the short circuits, hill climbs and sprint strips for years, with many a British and world record thrown in.

Gunga Din, the first of his three models, was evolved from a factory hack. Then, when George left the factory in 1951 to set up his own business, he went from strength to strength on Nero (unsupercharged) and Super Nero (supercharged). On these, he was free to make modifications forbidden on Gunga Din by factory policy. They included proprietary suspension, a lighter clutch, faster oil circulation and caged-roller big ends.

Designed for long life at normal revs, the standard crowded-roller big ends were inclined to jib at sustained high speeds – as I discovered to my embarrassment when the engine locked at about 130mph on the Montlhéry banking during a record bid at the Paris autodrome in 1952.

While George Brown was hogging the limelight in Britain, others were doing so elsewhere. Rollie Free set the ball rolling on the Bonneville Salt Flats in 1948, when he pushed the American record beyond 150 mph, lying prone on a Black Lightning in his bathing trunks. About the same time, René Milhoux chipped in with solo and sidecar records on a Belgian autoroute. But no achievement was more praiseworthy than that of Russell Wright and Robbie Burns on a damp, bumpy, 22ft-wide road near Christchurch, New Zealand, in July 1955. With their unblown Lightning enclosed in a homemade shell and pulling a 2·5-to-1 top gear, they pushed the world solo and sidecar records up to 185·15mph (Wright) and 163·06mph (Burns) respectively, winning the *Motor Cycle* trophy and £1000.

Final version of the Vincent twin was the 1955 Series D, with extensive weathershielding, Armstrong suspension struts and coil ignition. On a standard (Black Knight) model, I had no difficulty in packing 500 miles into eight hours one wet winter Sunday (during the 1954 London Show), although there were then no British motorways. What's more, petrol consumption averaged 53mpg, despite cruising speeds up to 100mph (no 70mph limit, either!).

But worldwide sales of expensive big bikes were taking repeated knocks from rising insurance, national bans, import quotas and market closures. Alas, the Vincent went down for the count.

With a frontal fairing to boost speed at the far end, George Brown spins off the line to start a standing kilometre on the Madiera Drive, Brighton

NSU Twins

Eager for prestige in the early 1950s, NSU decided to re-enter classic road racing to gain the worldwide fame that attends success. Failure they never contemplated. The right engineering approach, they reasoned, would ensure machines that would attract the top riders – an unbeatable combination. Sure enough, no other racing machine ever achieved such a swift, brief and shattering dominance of its class as did the 250cc Rennmax twin in 1953 and 1954.

Brushing aside the proud Moto-Guzzis, Werner Haas hogged the world championship in both years and spearheaded a sensational 1–2–3–4 in the 1954 Lightweight 250cc TT, adding an incredible 6mph to both lap and race records. Although his race speed exceeded 90mph, the NSU averaged no less than 42mpg. What's more, it won several grands prix at a higher speed than

that of the winning *three-fifty* at the same meeting.

Yet the Rennmax sprang from failure – the failure of a 500cc four built in 1951, when Germany was readmitted to the FIM following the war. Though that engine gave a creditable 53bhp, it was plagued by so many teething troubles that it was soon abandoned. Instead, a crankcase was made for one of its cylinders, to start the 125cc Rennfox on its world-conquering way. And the brilliant Dr Walter Froede (later engaged on Wankel research) grafted a pair of the four's cylinders on to the crankcase of a sports twin that had been shelved. That was the basis of the original Rennmax.

With a bore and stroke of 54mm, a pressed-up crankshaft supported in three main bearings, separate bevel drives to the two overhead camshafts, an enclosed pri-

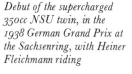

Debut of the supercharged 350cc NSU twin, in the 1938 German Grand Prix at the Sachsenring, with Heiner Fleichmann riding

mary chain and four speeds, it started off, in March 1972, with 27bhp at 9000rpm.

The splayed camshaft drives (on the right-hand side) were reminiscent of the blown 350cc twin that made its debut at the Sachsenring in August 1938. That cumbersome machine never got into its stride in the year before war broke out, but it fulfilled its promise afterwards when, in 1951, it collared the world 350cc and 500cc records at 172 mph and 180mph respectively on a German autobahn – then, in 1956, boosted those speeds to 189mph and 211mph on the

Bonneville salt flats in the USA.

By September 1952, six months after its debut, the Rennmax had been pepped-up to give 31bhp at 10400rpm, and it scared the daylights out of the Moto-Guzzi team when Haas finished the Italian Grand Prix at Monza only a tyre's breadth behind world-champion Enrico Lorenzetti, with Fergus Anderson (Lorenzetti's team-mate) beaten into third place.

The only significant changes for 1953 were a pressed-steel beam frame, with leading-link front fork, and a small fairing round the

steering head. Yet the Rennmax dominated all the classics except the TT, where newcomer Haas was only 17 seconds down on Fergus Anderson, and the Italian GP, where Lorenzetti sported a dolphin fairing for extra speed and beat Haas by 3·3 seconds.

The 1954 version of the Rennmax really broke the opposition's heart, for it reflected not only Dr Froede's appreciation of streamlining, but also his single-minded concentration on such fundamentals as filling the cylinders fully, burning the charge as efficiently as possible and minimising power losses from friction, pumping and distortion.

Besides adopting a peaked dolphin fairing (and, later, full frontal enclosure) Froede recast the engine extensively. To accommodate bigger inlet valves ($1\frac{9}{16}$in), ports and carburettors (28mm), and to reduce piston friction, the bore and stroke were altered to $55·9 \times 50·8$mm. Lengthening the connecting rods 10mm reduced the secondary out-of-balance forces.

Supported in four roller bearings, a five-

The engine that left the opposition gasping. Camshaft drive was by bevel gears to the inlet, then spur gears to the exhaust. Peak power on petrol was 39 bhp

piece forged crankshaft was designed, comprising a central power take-off and two complete 5in diameter flywheel assemblies – all clamped together by Hirth radially serrated couplings. The central gear drove a countershaft that served the clutch, ignition, oil pump and camshafts. On the left this time, a single bevel shaft drove the inlet camshaft, with a train of spur gears from there to the exhaust.

The cam boxes were integral with the massively finned heads, on to which air was deflected by a baffle plate under the tank. Included angle of the valves was only 50 degrees and the exhausts were sodium cooled.

In conjunction with a lift of 8mm and 30in long, shallow-taper megaphones, the valve timing was such that an airflow meter showed a theoretical breathing efficiency of 130 per cent. And since valve acceleration was crammed into the first quarter of the lift, the overlapping hairpin springs had no difficulty in preventing float should a gear be miscued.

Compression ratios between 8:1 and 11:1 were tried, and some secrecy surrounded the final shape of the combustion chambers, which at one stage were lopsided to concentrate the clearance volume around the sparking plug.

The six-volt coil ignition was unusual in having centrifugal auto-advance up to 5000 rpm, and a manual override by which the rider could shift the entire timing range. Because of the high speed at which the engine peaked (11500rpm), full advance was a hefty 40 degrees.

Another unusual feature was the method of getting oil to the big ends. It was squirted into annular channels in the adjacent faces of the inner flywheel discs, from where it centrifuged through drillways to the crankpins. Oil for the valve gear was fed via the hollow cam-lever spindles to the rubbing faces.

Although its running temperature was about 60 degrees C, the SAE20 oil was preheated to 90–100 degrees. Also preheated were the engines, through massive trunks from a hot-air blower that became a centre of attraction in every classic paddock. Transmission was through a dry clutch and six-speed gear cluster supported in needle-roller bearings.

Though the pre-race ritual may have seemed something of a pantomime, there was nothing comic about Rennmax performance in 1954. Engine power was quickly boosted from 33 to 39bhp, with a wonderful spread of torque from 5000 to 11500rpm. Top speed rocketed from 125mph in the TT (with dolphin fairing) to 135mph at Hockenheim (frontal enclosure). And with the speed there was always the utmost reliability.

The Rennmax simply left the opposition gasping. There wasn't a two-fifty to smell it.

MV Agusta four

Critics may talk about luck, and about MV Agusta's long supremacy in the world 500cc championship having to wait, as indeed it did, on Gilera's withdrawal in 1957 – but any machine that has won more titles in the class than all its rivals put together has earned its place in history. It is true that, before his switch to Yamaha, most of Giacomo Agostini's many MV successes were scored on the narrower, three-cylinder, 12-valve version. True, too, that the diminutive Carlo Ubbiali had already put the factory firmly on the lightweight map several years before Gilera's withdrawal left the 500cc class wide open to them. But the machines MV's renown was chiefly built on were the fours that carried John Surtees, Gary Hocking and Mike Hailwood to such an incredible succession of world championships.

The seeds of the four's success were sown when Britain's Les Graham joined MV at the end of 1950, for what was badly needed then to make the machine really competitive was the sang-froid and analytical flair of a top British or Commonwealth star. Already the engine was in the running for power, which was no surprise, since it was designed by Ing Pietro Remor, who had earlier designed the Gilera four, but the far superior handling of the British singles that then ruled the roost was something the Italians could only envy, not match.

When Graham arrived at the Gallarate factory, the machine was distinctly unorthodox. True the cylinders were set abreast across the frame, with the two overhead cam-

The 500cc MV Agusta in its early form, before Les Graham influenced development. Torsion sprung, the pivoted rear suspension has parallelogram linkage and friction damping. The girder fork has pressed-steel blades, and the sparking plugs are central

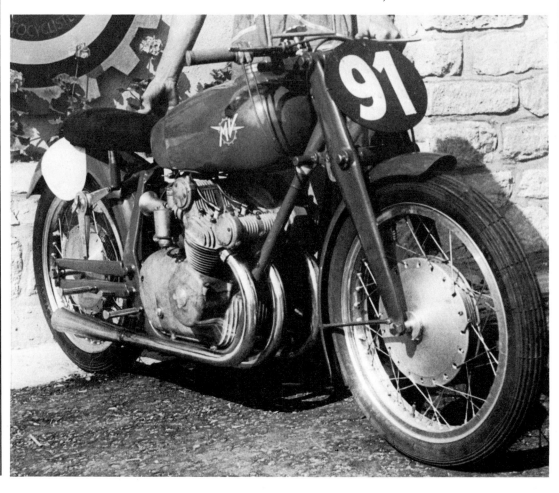

Left *Les Graham's first TT on the MV four – the 1951 Senior. Already the front fork is telescopic, the rear springing by proprietary struts and the plugs are inclined outward*

Below *Carlo Bandirola's machine at the 1952 Swiss Grand Prix, with chain drive and a single pivoted rear fork*

125

This Mettet shot of Les Graham clearly shows the layout of the pivoted front fork. Note, too, the arm recesses in the tank sides and the siamesed exhausts

shafts and the four-speed transmission driven from the middle of the crankshaft (indeed, the only apparent difference from the more familiar Gilera was that the sparking plugs were inclined outward, and were not central). But the drive was turned through 90 degrees at the gearbox to suit shaft-and-bevel final transmission on the left, and the pivoted rear suspension was doubled up, with one fork just above the other and the two linked together to form a parallelogram. Springing was by torsion bars and friction dampers.

Graham's first season on the MV four (1951) brought slim rewards. He found the handling poor, gear selection hit-and-miss (with the misses leading to bent valves), and the bike outsped by the Gileras, anyway. So big changes were made for 1952. The rear end of the bike bowed to convention, with chain drive and an orthodox pivoted fork, controlled by Girling spring-and-hydraulic struts. A fifth gear was added to the transmission. The exhaust pipes were siamesed on both sides. Most surprising of all, the telescopic front fork was replaced by an Earles-type pivoted fork with better damping but dubious geometry.

Graham's luck took a turn for the better. In the Senior TT he lay second to Geoff Duke's Norton for four laps, then finished runner-up to Reg Armstrong (Norton) in spite of losing 800rpm through a missed gear, and subsequently making an overlong pit stop. Later, in the Ulster Grand Prix, he led for half the race and set a record lap, only to strip the tread off the rear tyre when it fouled the mudguard on the notorious bumps of the seven-mile Clady straight. He finished the season in a blaze of glory by dominating the Italian and Spanish GPs from start to finish, even though he rode the last 20 of the 48 laps in Barcelona on only three cylinders, with one plug lead adrift.

If the writing was then on the wall, it was soon to become an obituary, for stark tragedy struck the following June, only a day after Graham had won the 1953 Lightweight 125 cc TT on an MV single, with record lap and race speeds. In the Senior race, while lying second to Geoff Duke (Gilera) just after the opening lap, he crashed fatally at the foot of

Bray Hill. But he had laid the foundations on which the MV legend was subsequently built.

It was 1956 before MV won a Senior TT and world championship – both by John Surtees, who brilliantly carried on Graham's development work in close liaison with the race-shop engineers. Save for 1957, when Gilera were invincible in their final year of classic racing, Surtees went on to notch a phenomenal string of 350/500cc grand prix doubles and world championships. On the big four he pioneered the hanging-in style of cornering, now almost universal, to keep the wide machine from grounding.

In turn, Gary Hocking and Mike Hailwood assumed the mantle of superstars on the all-conquering MV fours. But when Honda scaled up their wonderful two-fifty and began to trespass effectively on MV territory, the Italians changed to three cylinders to trim weight and width, switching to four-valve heads to keep the power up. Development eventually went full circle when the challenge of the two-stroke Yamahas forced MV back to four cylinders to find enough power and speed for Phil Read to keep the 500cc championship at Gallarate.

Moto-Guzzi single

If ever race engineering threw up a genius, he was Giulio Carcano. A man of fascinating personal charm as well as devastating logic, he relentlessly pursued his conviction that weight is evil – and not only in blunting acceleration, braking, climb and handling, but also in its effect on the rider's confidence.

When Moto-Guzzi quit classic racing at the end of 1957, Carcano's riders had taken the last five world 350cc championships on the lightest, lowest, slimmest and most beautifully streamlined machines ever to grace the start grids. With no more than 38bhp at the rear wheel, the final version – Keith Campbell's 1957 championship-winning flat single – was 15 to 20 per cent down on its rivals for power. But its weight was incredibly low at 216lb, including the full frontal fairing, and that weight was extraordinarily low slung.

Consequently the bike was more than competitive in acceleration and braking and could be whistled through bends faster and more easily than any other. Also its small frontal area and low drag coefficient gave it a top speed of about 140mph.

Lesser engineers have said that weight is necessary for road holding. Carcano's flat singles disproved it. They stuck to the ground by having the highest possible ratio of sprung to unsprung weight and really sensitive suspension, including leading-link front forks. When, in the mid 1950s, I tried out the TT-winning Moto-Guzzis on a stretch of the mountain road that was then quite rough, I got an uncanny impression of riding on a rail elevated an inch or two above the road, so unobtrusive was the springing for all the light weight.

There is a belief that a machine's race performance depends solely on its power-weight ratio – taking into account the fuel load and rider's weight – and that machines of substantially different weight and power would have equal performances provided the overall ratio was the same. Carcano's experiments showed this to be a fallacy.

Though the issue is complicated by variations in power characteristics, air drag and rolling resistance, generally the heaviest (hence most powerful) machine has the highest top speed, while the lightest (and

Bill Lomas rushing down the mountain on the beautifully streamlined 350cc Moto-Guzzi single to win the 1955 Junior TT. Note the ignition battery beneath the seat

Above left *evidence of Moto-Guzzi's open-minded approach was this straight four with shaft drive*

Above *another Moto-Guzzi experiment was quadruple hairpin valve springs on this early double-knocker engine*

least powerful) wins races, except on flat-out speed bowls. The reason they win is not just that they have an edge in acceleration, braking and handling. They also give the rider an easier time mentally, so that he corners consistently nearer the limit, confident he could win a wrestling match, should it be necessary.

There was nothing blinkered in Carcano's dedication to the featherweight flat single. No race engineer ever experimented with a wider variety of other types – a 120-degree vee-twin, a parallel twin, a shaft-drive four-in-line and a water-cooled vee-eight in two sizes, 350 and 500cc. Indeed, had the factory continued racing after 1957, they would most likely have switched to a horses-for-courses policy, racing the flat singles on give-and-take circuits and the eights on the ultra-fast ones.

Stepping up into the 350cc class was Fergus Anderson's brainwave in 1952. Since the parent five-speed two-fifty had just won its third world championship in four years, and its seventh TT (with another to come), he reasoned that boring and stroking the single-ohc engine would give him a fighting chance of 350cc honours.

So the engine was stretched from 68×68 mm to 72×80 mm (320cc). With power boosted from 28·5bhp at 8400rpm to 31 at 7700rpm, Anderson won the German Grand Prix at Hockenheim, before finishing third in the Junior TT to Ray Amm and Ken Kavanagh on the all-conquering works Nortons. Thus encouraged, Carcano built a full-size engine (75×79 mm) later in the season. That gave 33·5bhp at 7500rpm and a broad spread of torque. It ran into

teething troubles, but brought Anderson the world title he had envisaged.

By 1954 the bugs had been eliminated. A thicker cylinder liner and redesigned piston cured heavy oil consumption by eliminating distortion. Short big-end life was beaten by reverting from a one-piece crankshaft with a split, uncaged roller bearing, to a three-piece assembly with an ordinary caged-roller bearing. Anderson chalked up his second world championship.

Many changes were made for 1955. The cylinder liner was abandoned in favour of hard-chrome plating. Bore size was expanded to 80mm (stroke 69·5mm), while carburettor and valve sizes were increased to suit. Double overhead camshafts were adopted for valve-gear safety and with a modest hope of extra power. Ignition switched to battery and coils, with two 10mm plugs fired simultaneously. For the first time, the fairing went from dolphin to 'dustbin', with a space frame to suit. With 35bhp at 7800rpm, Bill Lomas took the world championship, then helped Anderson and Dickie Dale lift the 350cc hour record to 102·27 miles at Montlhéry.

Though Lomas hung on to his world title in 1956, Carcano was not satisfied. The bike's extra top speed had been achieved at the cost of bottom-end punch, and private tests on the twisty Modena circuit established that the 1954 single-knocker was faster both out of corners and in lap speed. So the priorities for 1957 were to boost low-speed torque and pare weight to the absolute safe minimum.

Cylinder dimensions reverted to 75×79 mm; valve sizes were slightly reduced; and the magneto was brought back, with a single

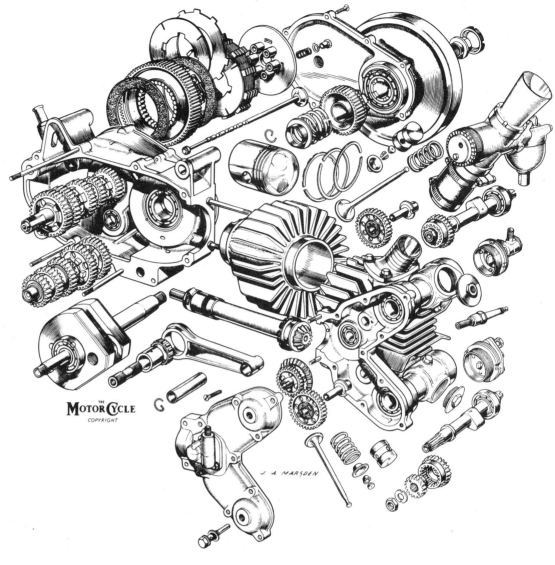

Engine of the world-conquering three-fifty in its final (1957) form. The crankshaft ran backward, and the light-alloy cylinder had a hard-chromed bore. Note the steep downdraught, single valve springs and outside flywheel. Running in oil, the steel-and-bronze clutch was virtually indestructible

THE
MOTOR CYCLE
COPYRIGHT

J. A. MARSDEN

Thrilled with his post-race impressions of Ken Kavanagh's 1956 Junior TT winner, the author stops for a word with race-chief Giulio Carcano. Kavanagh is on Willoughby's right

10mm plug, because dual ignition had required less advance, and if one plug fouled the engine went as flat as a pancake. Net result of the changes was a 3bhp increase in power (at 7800—8000rpm), with mechanical safety up to 8400rpm and a boost in torque so healthy that internal gear ratios were no longer changed to suit different circuits; and a total weight nearly 50lb lighter than the 264lb of the two-fifty from which the bike was developed in the first place.

The 1957 model was a honey in every way – easy to ride, easy to maintain. In keeping the world championship in Moto-Guzzi hands, Keith Campbell gave clear proof of Carcano's genius. For, on the tortuous Dutch TT circuit at Assen, he beat the formidable combination of Bob McIntyre and the Gilera four – the most tigerish rider on the most powerful machine. And he beat him simply because the Moto-Guzzi could be braked that much later, cornered that much faster. A week later, on the ultra-fast Belgian GP circuit at Francorchamps, Campbell again put it across Gilera, beating their home-bred star Libero Liberati by no less than 12·3 seconds.

To detail every instance of weight paring on the Moto-Guzzi is impossible. But it was typical of Carcano that he never used steel where aluminium was a feasible substitute, nor aluminium where the even lighter magnesium would do. And he chose single (coil) valve springs to save the weight of a few inches of wire, a 10mm plug because it was a shade lighter than a 14mm, and a hard-chromed cylinder bore to save the weight of an iron sleeve.

Race engineering threw up only one Giulio Carcano. Had it produced a dozen, that would not have been too many.

DKW three

The highest praise ever for DKW's three-cylinder two-stroke came from Fergus Anderson, shrewd manager of the rival Moto-Guzzi team. In the middle of the five-year span when his riders monopolised the world 350cc championship (1953 to 1957), Anderson said the title would have gone to the German five-speeder, save only for the brilliance of the Moto-Guzzi stars – particularly Bill Lomas, top dog in 1955 and 1956.

True enough, August Hobl had not only wrapped up the German championship on the 'Deek' as early as mid-1955, he had also harried Lomas in the classics, with speed and acceleration to spare. But the Italian team always had an edge in world-class riding talent, and their featherweight singles excelled in all-round race-worthiness.

Yet Anderson might well have gone further in his praise. For DKW had never made an unblown racing machine of any size before 1951, when West Germany was re-admitted to the FIM, and it was 1953 before the three made its debut. Its rapid rise to world class was a monument to the pains-taking work of Helmut Görg, who took over development in 1954 and still had some cards up his sleeve when the factory pulled out of racing at the end of 1956.

Founded by a Dane (I.S. Rasmussen) in 1921, DKW had clawed their way to the top of lightweight racing by the time war broke out in 1939, with a string of raucous, water-cooled two-strokes – all of them super-charged, the vast majority split singles – and again with developments in hand to meet any challenge to their supremacy.

The post-war partition of Germany brought the original factory at Zschopau, in Saxony, under Russian control. While that factory embarked on a new era as MZ (Motorradwerk Zschopau), DKW made a fresh start at Ingolstadt, in West Germany.

Their first unblown racer was an inclined 125cc single. And though its one and only piston committed it to symmetrical timing of the exhaust and transfer ports (unlike the pre-war split-single layout, page 98), the

1953 debut of the DKW 350cc three in Germany, with local star August Hobl aboard. Note the form-fitting tank

restrictions of symmetry were bypassed in the inlet timing by the use of a gear-driven cylindrical rotary valve at the rear of the crankcase. It was a simple step to double-up this engine to make a 250cc parallel twin with a long rotary valve across both crank chambers, fed by a carburettor at one end.

The drawback with that layout was the unequal lengths of the two inlet tracts. And the solution was to turn the rotor through 90 degrees, so that it lay fore-and-aft between the crank chambers. The carb fed the rear of the rotor, and the magneto protruded at the front, on the same axis. It was on this version of the two-fifty that Siegfried Wunsche, one of the factory's pre-war stars, had his final fling in the TT, finishing third in the 1953 Lightweight.

Meanwhile, DKW had become disenchanted with the cylindrical valve, which is inferior to the disc-type 'bacon-slicer' on several counts. A crankshaft-mounted disc not only requires no separate drive, it also gives more rapid port opening (hence

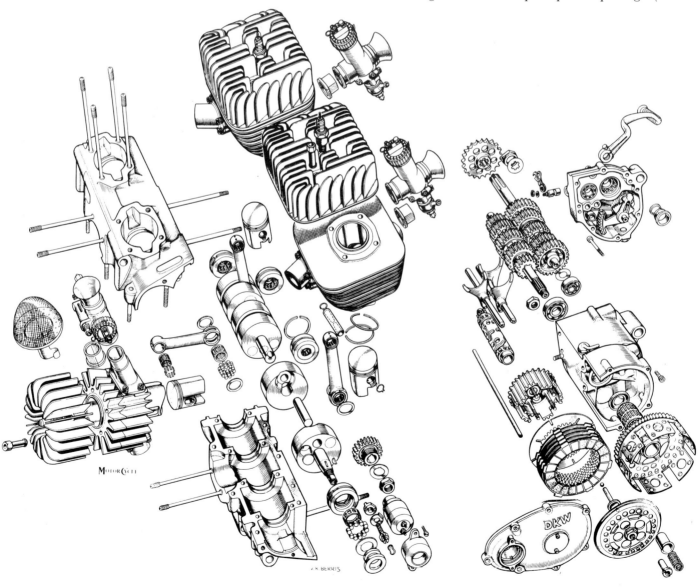

stronger pressure pulses) and a much shorter induction tract, with a higher natural resonant frequency which offers greater potential power.

But – unlike MZ at that very time – DKW did not clamber on the disc-valve band wagon. Instead, they simply abandoned the rotary valve, put a horizontal working cylinder (with longitudinal finning) in its place, and reduced the bore and stroke to 53 × 52·8mm to bring the total capacity within the 350cc limit. Hence, the peculiar cylinder arrangement, with the end ones sloping forward 15 degrees and the middle one flat, was just a quirk of development, never a design principle.

Indeed, it led to a strange crank arrangement. To simplify ignition, the designers wanted even firing intervals, which, with three cylinders in line, merely involves spacing the crankpins at 120 degrees to one another. But with the Deek's middle cylinder 75 degrees out of line with the others, only the outer pins were spaced at 120 degrees. The middle pin had to be only 45 degrees out of phase with the right-hand one.

Naturally, each cylinder had its own carburettor, and port timing was symmetrical all round. The displaced magneto, rehoused on the right-hand side of the crankcase, was a six-cylinder instrument driven at half engine speed.

At the outset, the three had an inadequate output of 31bhp and suspect reliability. Wunsche rode it in the 1953 Junior TT but retired. Yet within two years of taking over development the following March, Helmut Görg had boosted peak power to 45bhp at 9700rpm, top speed to 135–140mph (with a creditable fuel consumption of 30mpg), and achieved a level of reliability that was a byword. That sort of progress is an example of what top-level development engineering is all about.

Externally, the most apparent change was to six-volt battery-and-coil ignition, which slightly reduced power loss, cut rotating weight and gave fatter sparks. More crucial improvements were made internally, however – in bearing layout, shaft rigidity, port timing, piston and cylinder-head design and lubrication.

Housed in a light-alloy case where the magneto had been, the triple contact breaker was driven by a tongued plastic coupling. But though the shaft was at first supported in an outrigger bush in the cover as well as a ball bearing in the housing, fling of the cam lobe at speed upset the very critical timing. The solution was to lighten the lobe by extensive drilling and abandon the bush in favour of a long, double-row needle-roller bearing just inboard of the cam.

Cylinder porting was conventional for its time, with large ovals for the inlet and exhaust, and only two rectangular transfers directing their charge up the rear cylinder wall to the 12-to-1 squish head, in which the half-moon segment was at the front. But hand grinding of the ports lacked the necessary consistency, so internal and external grinding jigs were made for fitting to the cylinder jackets and liners respectively. After port timing was checked with a protractor, cylinders were individually matched for power before being built into a unit.

Bottom-end reliability came from enlarging the four roller main bearings; beefing-up the six-piece pressed crankshaft (aligned to an incredible accuracy of 0·001mm); changing from rubber to metal gas seals and from floating small-end bushes to caged needle rollers; and finally directing the fresh charge towards the big ends – which made it possible to reduce the proportion of oil in the petrol from six per cent to four.

Aids to power included heat-resistant plastic mounting sleeves and warm-air deflector plates for the 28mm Dellorto carburettors (to keep the charge as cool and dense as possible); the barest running clearance for the flywheel discs, and less than $\frac{1}{4}$in gaps for the slim connecting rods (to give a high primary compression ratio); and some of the earliest resonant exhaust boxes (flattened for cornering clearance) to improve cylinder scavenging and filling.

The normal power band was from 7500 to 11000rpm. But so freely would the turbine-smooth engine rev beyond the safe limit of 15000rpm that Görg had 'dead' pointers fitted to the rev-counters. These showed the highest revs reached, and, to the occasional embarrassment of the riders, could be returned to zero only with a magnet.

Top speed without a fairing approached 120mph, and a further 20mph came from a frontal fairing evolved in the wind tunnel at Munich Technical College. This substantial reduction in wind resistance, coupled with the very mild overrun braking effect of the engine, led to the use of four 9½in-diameter double-leading-shoe brakes, all hydraulically operated from the pedal, with a supplementary hand lever for the front ones.

The real pity of DKW's withdrawal from racing when the three was so competitive was that Görg was convinced the engine's all-round efficiency could have been improved 15 per cent by petrol injection. . . .

When the horizontal cylinder was added to the parallel two, the magneto (a six-cylinder instrument driven at half engine speed) was moved to the right-hand side of the crankcase

Exploded view of the three-cylinder engine in its final (1956) form. Cylinder and head finning were matched to the airflow. Porting was conventional, with piston control for the inlets. Roller bearings were used for the mains, big ends and small ends. Primary drive was by gears. Note the unusual shape of the air-intake gauzes

AJS Boy Racer

Six years of painstaking toil and experiment by development engineer Jack Williams boosted the peak power of the 350cc single-ohc AJS 7R from 37bhp at 7500rpm, at the end of 1954, to nearly 42 at 7800 (while cutting its weight from 310 to 285lb), to make it one of the most popular and successful racers ever marketed. It is all the more ironical, then, that the only version of the so-called Boy Racer to hit the jackpot by winning a TT (1954 Junior, Rod Coleman) was the experimental three-valver, shelved when the factory quit official racing shortly before Williams joined them.

Williams' brief was as daunting as his achievement was prodigious. It was to squeeze the last ounce of power from an unsophisticated design without exceeding a budget that amounted to a straitjacket or pricing the machine out of the market.

The 7R had already been available since early 1948, when it was initially regarded as a fairly unblushing copy of the Mk VIII KTT Velocette. It had the Velo's bore and stroke (74×81mm), its eccentric rocker spindles (for valve-clearance adjustment), pivoted-fork rear springing and magnesium-alloy cone hubs.

Its chief difference from the KTT lay in the use of a ⅜in-pitch Weller-tensioned chain to drive the camshaft. The Boy Racer also had a telescopic, not girder, front fork, and spring-and-hydraulic rear-suspension struts rather than Dowty oleo-pneumatics. What's more, it was appreciably lighter than the Velo – thanks to a welded frame and the

Sectioned drawing of the AJS 7R, one of the most popular 350cc racers ever marketed. It was developed by Jack Williams on an extremely restrictive budget

Bob McIntyre, the rider who put the 7R on the map by winning the 1952 Junior Manx Grand Prix. Two days later he brought the same three-fifty home second in the Senior

Rod Coleman on the first three-valve version during practice for the 1952 Swiss Grand Prix. Two years later he won the Junior TT on it

extensive use of magnesium for the engine castings and aluminium for the tanks.

Since 72-octane was the only petrol available in 1948, compression ratio was originally a modest 8·45:1. The engine peaked at 6800 to 7000rpm.

By the time Jack Williams took over development, the two-valve 7R's most spectacular success was Bob McIntyre's emphatic win in the 1952 Junior Manx Grand Prix, followed two days later by a brilliant second place in the Senior *on the same machine.* Realising there was not a great deal more in the rpm kitty, Williams immediately got busy boosting the punch of each individual power impulse (in engineering terms, in-

creasing the brake mean effective pressure).

Using a wooden cylinder head dummy with different inlet port shapes, he soon found that the port that passed the most gas didn't give the most power. By concentrating the petrol spray from the jet instead of mixing it thoroughly with the air, it lost some neat fuel to the exhaust and failed to burn the rest to the best advantage.

A port promoting more turbulence gave an extra $1\frac{1}{2}$bhp in spite of passing less gas. A third port shape, which gave a tangential swirl to the ingoing gases, pushed the power up another $1\frac{1}{2}$bhp to 40.

Test rigs were also used to determine the best size and shape for the inlet valve, and

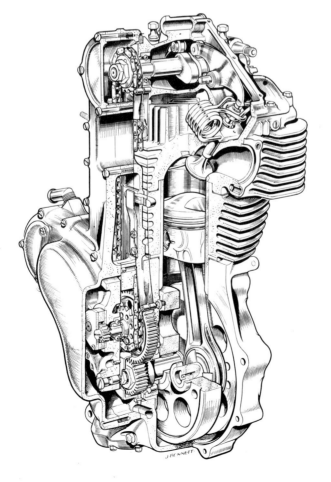

the optimum length and diameter of the induction tract. This work spread the useful power band from 5200 to 7800rpm. Experiments on the angle of the exhaust port resulted in a 10-degree offset, which marginally increased both power and fuel consumption.

Next, a squish-type combustion chamber, with a flat piston crown, promoted still more turbulence while giving a much more compact shape at top dead centre. This enabled the compression ratio to be stepped up from 10·8:1 to 12·2:1, and the quicker combustion was reflected in a cut-back in ignition advance from 37 to 34 degrees.

By that time, peak power was 41bhp at 7800rpm. And since the bmep was an almost unprecedented 210psi, the search for more punch was called off. Instead, attention was focussed on inlet cam design, since the rpm limit was set by breakage of the inlet valve springs due, as stroboscopic tests showed, to surge.

The first viable new cam banished spring surge beyond 8000rpm, and gave 41·5bhp at 7800rpm. But it needed springs so strong that they quickly succumbed to overstressing. Finally, a cam was designed to give the valve much fiercer initial acceleration, so

138

allowing the springs more time to do their job of slowing and returning the valve.

Though this cam brought the onset of spring surge down to 7900rpm, there were ample compensations. First, weaker springs could be used, and that solved the breakage problem. Second, the sharper initial valve opening (and final closing) gave a 3 per cent bmep improvement in the very useful rev range from 6000 to 7500rpm.

Considering his very restrictive terms of reference, Jack Williams had worked wonders. For the simple two-valve production engine finished up as a more powerful unit than the works TT-winning three-valver that, albeit undeveloped, started off with a built-in advantage.

Designed in 1952 by Ike Hatch (earlier concerned with the four-valve Excelsior Mechanical Marvel), the 7R3A ended a five-year run of Norton victories in the Junior TT when Rod Coleman won the 1954 five-lapper non-stop. Only a month later, a much-modified version (the 7R3B) was completed, giving 39 to 40bhp at 8000rpm. But the factory's change of policy prevented it from being raced.

The A and B versions differed chiefly in the complex drive to the camshafts. In the A layout, the camshaft for the single inlet valve was directly driven by chain. A spur gear on the camshaft drove a cross shaft in front of it. Finally, bevel gears at the ends of the cross shaft drove fore-and-aft sloping camshafts for the two exhaust valves.

Unfortunately, the fixed centres for the chain sprockets meant that different compression ratios could be tried only by changing the piston-crown height. So the chain was abandoned in favour of bevel gears and a vertical shaft. Compression could then be altered by varying the thickness of shims under the cylinder, and adjusting the shaft length by fitting thinner or thicker Oldham couplings.

In the B arrangement, the top vertical bevel meshed with a compound gear from which the drive went up to the cross-shaft serving the exhaust camshafts, then back to the inlet shaft. As in the two-valve engine, the inlet valve had overlapping hairpin springs, but the exhausts had triple coils.

Hatch's aims in doubling-up the exhaust valves were several. First, two small valves run cooler than a large one, so heating the incoming charge less; the denser charge increases power. Second, the sparking plug can be put practically in the middle of the cylinder head, so shortening flame travel. Third, the exhaust ports can be widely

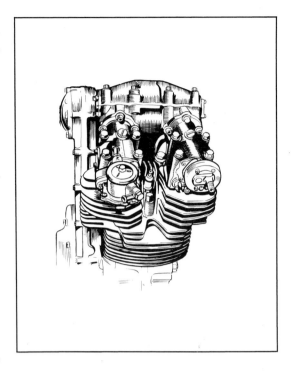

In Rod Coleman's TT-winning engine the inlet camshaft was chain-driven From a cross-shaft, bevel gears drove the two exhaust camshafts

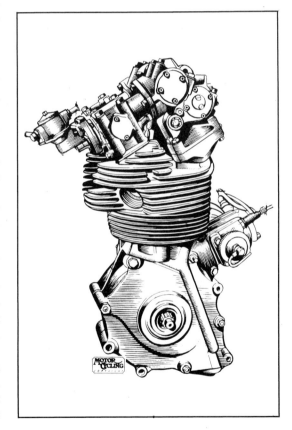

Never raced, the 7R3B engine had the overhead cam mechanism driven by a vertical shaft and bevel gears (on the remote side in this view). Peak power was 40bhp at 8000rpm

splayed, leaving plenty of room for cooling fins. Finally, light valves don't float so readily as heavy ones. Since the engine gave 2bhp more than the two-valver with the same inlet-valve and port sizes, the theory seemed to be vindicated.

If only Jack Williams had been allowed to devote his efforts to the three-valver as well as the two, the competitive life of the British racing single might well have been extended.

BSA Gold Star

The renown of the BSA Gold Star rests chiefly on its dominance of the Isle of Man Clubman's TT races in the 1950s, but it was a very versatile model – being supplied for fast touring, trials riding, scrambling and track racing. Its origin dates back to 1937, when on the last day of June Wal Handley won a Brooklands Gold Star for lapping at over 100mph on a 500cc iron-engined Empire Star specially prepared to run on alcohol by Jack Amott and Len Crisp. Handley's race-winning speed was 102·27 mph, his best lap 105·57mph – and the name Empire Star was naturally changed to Gold Star for the revamped 1938 model.

Though the name Empire Star was first applied to the sports five-hundred in 1936, that year's model was virtually the earlier Blue Star, which had the magneto in front of the cylinder, the oil compartment integral with the crankcase, and a forged-steel beam for the top frame member. It was in 1937 that Val Page took over design and gave the Empire Star a new identity. He separated the oil tank from the crankcase and put a worm-driven, gear-type oil pump in the famous crankcase bulge that called for the cranking of the right-hand engine-cradle tube. The valves were enclosed, and the pushrods housed in a single tapered tower;

the magneto was shifted behind the cylinder and the frame beam abandoned in favour of orthodox tubular construction.

That was the basis of Handley's Brooklands racer, but many changes were made by the time the Gold Star was catalogued in 1938, with a choice of standard, competition or track trim. Light alloy was used for the cylinder and head, with screwed-in valve seats. The pushrod tower was an integral part of the castings. An Amal TT carburettor was standardised and, most surprising of all, the gearbox shell was cast in magnesium alloy. Common or garden aluminium was used for the shell in 1939, although there was then an option of a close-ratio gear cluster. That was the last of the Gold Star for nine years – during which its modest cousin, the M20 side-valve, did valiant war service.

When the Gold Star reappeared in 1948, it was as a three-fifty with a bore and stroke of 71 × 88mm, and the same stroke was retained (with an 85mm bore) for the later five-hundred. Naturally, in view of Bill Nicholson's phenomenal run of successes in trials and scrambles, it was in those guises that the three-fifty made its debut. The racing version was introduced later to meet the challenge of the Clubman's TT. This high degree of versatility was achieved by

The original BSA Gold Star – a 1938 five-hundred based on Wal Handley's Brooklands Gold Star-winning Empire Star

Opposite 1952 racing version of the BSA Gold Star engine, with which Eric Houseley won the 1952 Clubman's Junior TT. Note the outrigger plate for the timing gears, the cast-in pushrod tunnel and the worm-driven oil pump in the crankcase

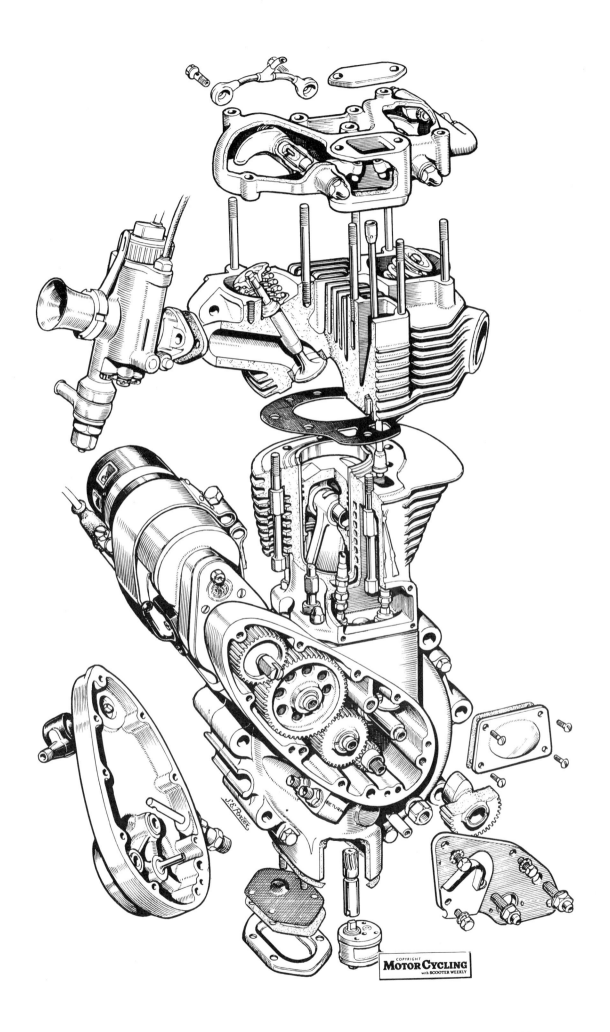

ringing the changes on valve and port sizes (different cylinder heads were available) and on cams and pistons.

Straightforward and robust, the new engine followed the broad lines of the pre-war five-hundred, albeit incorporating the fruits of a good deal of fresh thinking and experimental work on the part of Bert Hopwood, then BSA's chief designer. To steepen the inlet downdraught and so ease the gas path into the cylinder, the included angle of

the valves was narrowed from 75 to 66 degrees. This also reduced the depth of the head recess and, in conjunction with a flat piston crown, gave a more compact combustion space. Total bonus from the head alterations was claimed to be $2\frac{1}{2}$ bhp.

To keep down production costs, the die-cast Y-alloy cylinder head was separate from its rocker box. The method of inserting the austenitic-steel valve seats was changed to pressing and shrinking. At 1·6in diameter,

Above *Ulsterman Billy Nicholson, once supreme in trials and scrambles on BSA Gold Stars. Here he is in the 1952 Manville Cup Trial*

Right *in the last year of the Isle of Man Clubman's TT (1956), Bernard Codd scored a double. Here he rounds Signpost Corner in the Senior event*

the racing inlet valve was the largest that could be accommodated, and necessitated cutting away the top of the cylinder bore. Nimonic 80, a nickel alloy from a range developed for gas turbines, was chosen for the exhaust valve.

No fewer than five cams were available to suit the engine's different guises. For comparison, the clubman-racing cam gave a total inlet period of 325 degrees and a lift of 0·410in, against 270 degrees and 0·300in for the trials cam. Overlap with the racing cam was 115 degrees compared with 88 degrees for the tourer – and even that was much greater than the 50 degrees of the standard B31 350cc roadster. Both inlet and exhaust tracts were tuned, with the result that engine speed had to be kept above 4000rpm for the overlap to be fully effective.

Besides four long bolts reaching right up from the crankcase, there were four shorter ones clamping the head to the barrel. The one-piece valve rockers were hardened in the bore and ran on hardened spindles, an unusual arrangement.

Another departure from B31 dimensions was a $\frac{1}{2}$in shortening of the forged-steel connecting rod (in 1952). The idea was threefold – to lower engine height, reduce the rod's inertia and improve combustion efficiency by moving the piston more rapidly through the top-dead-centre position. Smoother running vindicated the theory. Also forged were the polished flywheels, which were clamped to the crankpin against both tapers and shoulders, and had the flanged mainshafts pressed in and riveted from the inside.

In addition to two roller main bearings hard up against the wheels, there was a ball bearing on the drive side and a bronze bush on the timing side. Instead of live spindles running in bushes in the timing cover, there was an outrigger plate supporting fixed spindles for the camwheels and idler, so that the cover took no load and meshing could be checked before it was screwed on, and blind assembly avoided.

Every new Gold Star was supplied with a certificate of engine performance. Average bhp figures were 18 at 5500rpm for the trials engine (compression ratio only 6·5:1), 27·5 at 6800 for the clubman racer (9:1) and 30·5 at the same revs for the track racer (13:1).

In the later years of Gold Star production the trials and scrambles versions were dropped. And the very dominance of the racing version in the Clubman's TT was instrumental in that event being dropped in 1957. The last Goldie was produced in 1962 – and the model is still mourned.

Desmodromic Ducati

In resurrecting the four-valve cylinder head from 25 years of neglect in the early 1960s, Honda solved the pressing problem of valve control at ultra-high revs and profoundly influenced the subsequent course of four-stroke racing-engine development. But more than a dozen years earlier Ing Fabio Taglioni had found a different solution to valve float, with his ingenious desmodromic valve gear. All that prevented him from stealing Honda's thunder and steering design away from valve springs altogether was the lack of resources to put his ideas into practice.

Six years later, in 1954, Taglioni joined Ducati at Bologna, in his native Italy. Within a year he had built his first desmodromic engine (with cams to close the valves as well as open them). A year later still, the engine made its debut in the 1956 Swedish Grand Prix at Hedemora, where Taglioni's theories were immediately vindicated when Degli Antoni won the 125cc race so convincingly

that he lapped every other rider. Yet that was nothing to the humiliation the new Ducati was to heap on the MV Agustas and FB Mondials that had been sitting pretty for so long at the top of the 125cc heap.

By the late 1950s, valve springs were nearing the end of their tether on high-compression, two-valve 125cc singles. So close were valve-to-piston clearances that a brief bout of over-revving, whether caused by a missed gear or a moment's inattention to the rev-counter, could bring instant engine failure through bent valves. Taglioni's positive valve closure not only pushed the Ducati's safe revs way up to 14000rpm; it also enabled higher valve lifts to be used, which boosted peak power from 16bhp at 12000 rpm to 19bhp at 12500rpm.

The 112-mph desmodromic single (55·25 × 52mm) made its Isle of Man TT debut in 1958, and until the engine went sick Luigi Taveri showed Carlo Ubbiali, MV's estab-

On the Isle of Man Clypse circuit in 1958, Luigi Taveri uses the desmo Ducati's speed to lead world champion Carlo Ubbiali (MV Agusta) in the Lightweight 125cc TT

lished superstar, the way round. Even then, Ubbiali was chased home by three more desmos, ridden by Romolo Ferri, Dave Chadwick and Sammy Miller. The writing was on the wall.

Worse was soon to come for MV. On the ultra-fast Belgian and Swedish GP circuits, where a deficiency in engine power could not easily be cancelled out by superior cornering, the Ducati riders trounced them. In Belgium, MV's fiery Tarquinio Provini was beaten into third place by Ducati's

four cams mounted on a single shaft, the racers of the late 1950s had three camshafts. Conventionally, the valve-opening cams were at the front and rear of the integral cam-box, and they actuated the valves through pivoted levers. The peculiar-looking closing cams were on the middle shaft (driven by bevel gears) and they actuated the valves through forked rockers bearing on the underside of flanged collars.

Reason for the three-shaft layout was that the desmo head was developed from the

Alberto Gandossi and Romolo Ferri. In Sweden, Gandossi and Luigi Taveri did the same to Carlo Ubbiali.

MV staked everything on a comeback in the Italian GP at Monza and were slaughtered. Desmos – four singles and a new 118-mph twin pushing out 22·5 bhp at 14000rpm (and safe to 17000) – filled the first five places. Both Ubbiali and Provini wrecked their engines in the vain chase; the only MV works rider to finish, Enzo Vezzalini in sixth place, was lapped.

Unlike the latest Ducati vee-twin roadsters, in which each cylinder head has its

twin-ohc head of the catalogued Grand Prix racer, which had hairpin valve springs. Indeed, the works desmodromic models were virtually standard from the cylinder head downward – and the desmo head would fit not only the Grand Prix but also the Formula 3 model, which normally had a single camshaft and rockers. Further evidence of the standard nature of the lower part of the engine was the kick-starter boss in the left-side crankcase casting and a vacant space on the same side of the crankshaft, where the roadsters carried the generator. Also, only four pairs of transmission gears were situated

Dave Chadwick, third in the 1958 Lightweight 125cc TT on one of the three desmos that chased Carlo Ubbiali home

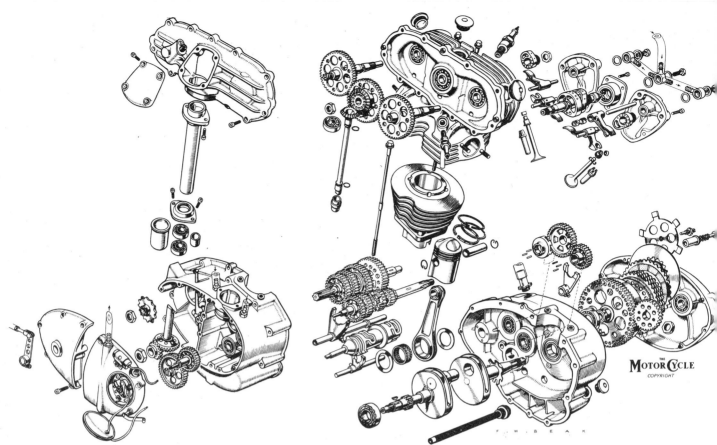

The Motor Cycle
COPYRIGHT

F. W. BEAK

Above *exploded drawing of the single-cylinder engine. The front and rear camshafts opened the valves, the middle one closed them. The fifth-gear pinions were sandwiched behind the clutch*

Right *standard from the cylinder-head joint downward, the desmo engine had a second sparking plug in front of the upper bevel box*

Photographed during a Silverstone tryout in 1960, Mike Hailwood's 350cc parallel-twin desmo Ducati

in the main compartment between the crank-case walls. The other pair or pairs (according to whether the machine was a five or six-speeder) were in the primary-drive compart-ment, inboard of the clutch.

Naturally, it was impossible to design or machine closing cams that would just hold the valves on their seats at all engine temperatures without ever overloading the rubbing surfaces. The simple answer was for the cams to close the valves to within about 0·012in of their seats and let valve inertia and cylinder pressure do the rest. At first, light rocker-return springs were fitted to ensure full compression at very low rpm. But when they were discarded, for fear of the damage that could be caused by a broken spring, there was no difference in the running of the engine. The only effect was seemingly poor compression if the engine was turned very slowly by hand, though the valves sealed perfectly at push-starting speeds.

Of course, if a sizeable piece of grit was sucked through the carburettor and trapped under the inlet valve something had to give, but Taglioni decided to take that risk rather than fit an air filter, which would have restricted the engine's breathing. Another theoretical snag was that the reciprocating weight of the valve gear was slightly greater than in the double-knocker engine; conse-quently the inertia forces were higher, especially in view of the higher rpm used and the fiercer cam contours. The important thing, however, was that the inertia could not cause the valves to fling, as when springs are used to close them.

Sound, though fairly orthodox, engineer-ing characterised the rest of the power plant. To spread tooth loading in the camshaft drive, the hunting-tooth principle was used for the bevel gears – the numbers of teeth, from the crankshaft upward, being 21, 30, 20 and 28. There was an integral half-gallon oil sump, which served the transmission as well as the engine. Carburettor size was 27mm for most circuits, though it went up to 29mm for the ultra-fast ones and down to 22 for the really tiddly national ones. On average, petrol consumption was 45mpg.

On the single there were two sparking plugs (one 14mm, the other 10), fired by separate three-volt coils and a common six-volt battery. Compression was about 10:1 (10·2 for the twin).

After the Monza massacre of 1958, Ducati's hopes for the following year were frustrated by injuries to their star rider, Bruno Spaggiari. Then, with a four-cylinder engine on the stocks (as well as the 42·5 × 45mm twin) a change in factory policy put a brake on their racing activity just when desmodromics were poised to consolidate. Anyway, in the long term, Honda's four-valve layout had the edge. For it not only solved the problem of valve float; it also passed more gas, gave more thorough turbu-lence and allowed the plug to be put smack in the middle of the head for the shortest possible flame path.

Even so, Taglioni's was a wonderful achievement. For the only other concern to make a success of desmodromics was Mercedes-Benz, in car racing – and the German company's resources made Ducati's look like peanuts.

MZ two-stroke

When supercharging was banned for classic racing after the war, few would have given a fig for the two-stroke's chances. Among the few was Walter Kaaden, racing and development chief for MZ, in East Germany. Everyone knew that DKW owed their immediate pre-war dominance of the 250 and 350cc classes to supercharging. Without it, how could the humble two-stroke hold a candle to the four-stroke?

Working at the same Zschopau factory that had produced the ear-splitting DKWs in the 1930s, Kaaden, almost alone, recognised that a two-stroke was not so much a pumping engine – with the piston pulling in the fresh charge and pushing out the burnt – as a resonant device, just as organ pipes were way back when the only prime mover known to man was fuelled with hay.

Trained as an engineer at Chemnitz before the war, Kaaden had raced two-strokes he made himself before joining MZ at the end of 1952. From the start there, he pinned his faith on disc inlet valves rather than piston-controlled ports. That way, the inlet timing could be asymmetric, and he could get a much longer induction period without the late closing that results in blowback through the carburettor. Within a few years his 125cc single and 250cc twin matched the best, and top Western stars were clamouring to ride them.

In 1959, Luigi Taveri had the 125cc TT in his pocket when an overtight helmet gave him double vision towards the end, and his easing of the pace led to plug fouling and let Tarquinio Provini through on the MV Agusta.

Straddling the MZs in only the second half of the season, up-and-coming Gary Hocking romped to four brilliant wins, including the 250cc Swedish and Ulster GPs, and finished runner-up in the world championship to Carlo Ubbiali (MV Agusta), who had been piling up points all season. In the Italian GP at Monza MZ's home-bred star, Ernst Degner, beat Ubbiali in the 125cc race, and was a mere wheel's breadth behind him on the twin.

Both lightweight titles were a racing certainty for Hocking and MZ the following year. But Count Agusta recognised the threat and bought Hocking with Western currency that MZ could not offer.

In the Italian 250cc Grand Prix at Monza in 1959, Ernst Degner's MZ twin leads Carlo Ubbiali's MV Agusta. Ubbiali won by a wheel, but Degner beat him in the 125cc race

Undeterred, Kaaden hit the jackpot in 1961 with the first-ever 200bhp/litre power unit (25bhp at 10800rpm from the one-two-five). Degner was leading the world 125cc championship by two points with only the Argentine GP to go, but at that crucial time he defected to the West, was barred from riding the MZ in Argentina – and the title went to Tom Phillis (Honda) by default. With occasional outings in subsequent years, Mike Hailwood and Alan Shepherd proved the MZs at least a match for the Hondas which had then taken over from MV Agusta as top lightweights.

Yet, for all his inability to retain Western stars, his shoestring budget and pitiful shortage of resources, Kaaden had evolved the formula that was to be the basis for the vast majority of Suzuki's and Yamaha's TT and world-championship successes from 1962 onward. For when Degner fled from Communism he took his know-how to Japan, where first Suzuki and then Yamaha spent a fortune refining the MZ formula without

Ernst Degner in the 1960 German 250cc Grand Prix at Solitude. He retired with carburettor flooding when well placed

Impeccable style by Alan Shepherd while winning the 1964 American 250cc Grand Prix at Daytona

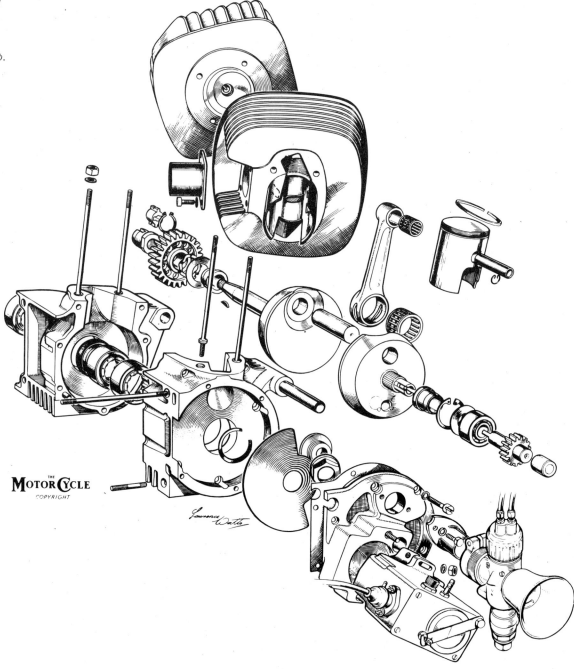

Mechanical simplicity and well harnessed resonances characterised the 1961 air-cooled MZ single, first one-two-five to reach 25 bhp. Note the half-moon squish band, short exhaust port, single piston ring, needle-roller con-rod bearings and cutaway inlet disc

being able to improve it one iota.

Basically, the formula is simple: a short, highly resonant induction tract, with a disc valve in the crankcase wall; an auxiliary transfer port (or ports) opposite the exhaust, besides the usual two at the sides; a squish-type combustion chamber; and a highly resonant exhaust system (preferably in the rear cylinder wall relative to crankshaft rotation, the better to seal the crankcase from the exhaust port).

Calculations, even taking account of gas speed and temperature, were found to be only a starting point in seeking the optimum dimensions for the exhaust system. From there on, it was a case of painstaking experiments, as with induction and transfer.

Kaaden's achievement in harnessing the natural resonances was proved by failures as well as successes. For when an exhaust box split during a race, the engine power evaporated. When an inlet disc jammed wide open at full power on bench test, the engine continued to run unimpaired until the throttle was closed.

MZ's first racer, in 1953, was a three-speed 125cc single with two conical exhaust pipes at the rear and only two transfer ports. Starting the season with 9bhp at 7800rpm, it finished with 11·75bhp as a result of larger transfer and exhaust ports, a higher compression ratio and changes in the length and taper of the exhaust pipes.

For 1954 it was given four speeds, tuned to

13bhp at 8000rpm and partnered by a 250 cc twin. This was virtually a pair of 125cc engines with the inner ends of their crankshafts splined into a common driving gear. All development work was done on the single and subsequently incorporated in the twin.

About that time, a couple of abortive experiments were abandoned when the 125 cc engines gave only 12bhp at 9000rpm. One was a parallel twin. The other was an opposed-piston single with a crankcase and carburettor at each end. The transfer ports were at the bottom end of the cylinder, the exhausts at the top (uniflow), and the exhaust piston was given a 15-degree lead so that it both opened and closed its ports before the transfers. But the scheme foundered on the excessive length of the transfer passages from the top crankcase.

The crude beginnings of the modern complex exhaust box were seen in 1955, with a single pipe and a baffled outlet. The aim was not only to produce a depression at the exhaust port during the transfer phase, but also to prevent loss of charge to the exhaust by reflecting back a positive pressure wave just before the port closed. As a result, peak power went up to 15bhp at 9000rpm, and the riders began to win national and international races.

But the power band had become too narrow for four speeds, and the high revs overtaxed the bearings and magneto. With a six-speed gear cluster for 1956, however, a needle-roller small-end bearing and battery ignition, the bikes then had 16·5bhp at 9200rpm.

Then came the last of the abortive experiments – a 125cc single with a horizontal cylinder and a skew-driven disc on top of the crankcase, feeding cool mixture straight over the big end. But the piston seized, the skew gears failed and the shielded crankcase heated the charge so much that 14bhp was top whack anyway.

From then on, intensive development of the established layout yielded an average (though declining) boost of nearly 2bhp a year – the biggest single gain (1½bhp) coming from the third transfer port, fed through a window high in the piston skirt. Oddly enough, the port was not introduced for power but to ease the arduous lot of the small end beyond 10000rpm, by passing some cool, oily gas over it on its way up to the cylinder.

As the engine's peak revs climbed to 12000rpm, all three port durations (inlet, transfer and exhaust) had to be extended, for they are based on time, not crank angle.

Eventually crankcase filling became so efficient (some 105 to 110 per cent of the swept volume) that the primary compression ratio had to be reduced from 1·6:1 to 1·5:1, simply to make room for the extra charge rather than blow it back through the carburettor.

There may be no tangible reward for evolving a world-beating formula for wealthier companies to exploit. But Walter Kaaden's MZs were the finest grand prix machines never to win a TT or world championship.

Top *the 250cc twin was virtually two 125cc singles coupled to a central driving gear.*

Above *water-cooled version of the twin, with half-speed magneto*

Honda four

Honda's debut in classic road racing was so mediocre it gave not the slightest hint of the overwhelming dominance the Japanese company was soon to achieve in all five solo classes of the world championships. In the spring of 1959 they traipsed halfway round the world to western Europe with a handful of old-fashioned-looking 125cc six-speed twins that plainly lacked the pace of the MV, Ducati and MZ singles. Nor had their home-bred riders anything like the verve of the European stars.

No one could possibly have guessed that Honda would quit the tracks only nine years later with a bag of 18 manufacturers' world championships, 16 individual titles, 18 Isle of Man TTs (among a total of 137 grands prix) – and an astonishing record of technical innovation and quick-fire engine development in the face of repeated fierce two-stroke challenges.

Immaculately prepared though those original twins unquestionably were, they incorporated several features long since abandoned by western race engineers – flat throttle slides, pivoted front suspension, larger front wheel than rear, and four valves per cylinder. And though the machines proved reliable enough to finish sixth, seventh and eighth in the Lighweight 125cc TT, so earning Honda the manufacturers' team prize, their whole effort was greeted with amused condescension, if not outright derision.

This scepticism was reinforced a year later, when they duplicated their 125cc TT showing (though missing the team prize) and the best of their new 250cc fours, even in the capable hands of Australian Bob Brown, could finish no higher than fourth, easily outpaced by a brace of MV twins and a Moto-Morini single.

The 1961 250cc Honda four that hit the racing world like a bombshell. Revving to 14000rpm, this 16-valver swamped both the TT and the world championship

To strengthen the team, two more Commonwealth riders – Jim Redman and Tom Phillis – were recruited, but the Japanese bikes were still trounced by the Italians for the rest of the season. But when Honda went quietly home, it was not to lick their wounds. It was to sort out the tantrums that had plagued the engines at top revs and to find more power. That was the calm before the storm.

The 1961 Lightweight TTs, both 250 and 125cc, were massacres. Hondas swamped the first five places in each, with Mike Hailwood winning both. But it was Bob McIntyre who showed what the two-fifty was really capable of. Plagued throughout practising and the warm-up by oil leakage and excessive oil temperature, as a result of the switch from an integral sump to a separate tank, he knew it was touch and go whether the supply would see him through.

But he rode that Honda as no man had before and none but Hailwood has since. Enthralling the crowds everywhere with a magnificent display of courage and skill, accompanied by the haunting howl of a 14000rpm megaphone quartet, he set such a pace that his opening lap lopped no less than 48·4 seconds off Carlo Ubbiali's record and gained a lead of nearly half a minute on MV's brilliant new star, Gary Hocking.

Mac's next lap bettered even John Surtees' 350cc record (set on an MV four) and, at 99·58mph, came within a few seconds of the magic ton. Yet all the time his left-hand cornering was cramped by oil on the rear tyre. Eventually, with no one else in the hunt, Mac's engine seized for want of oil at the Quarry Bends, halfway round the final lap, leaving Hailwood a grateful winner from Phillis and Redman.

Hailwood finished the season as world 250cc champion, Phillis as 125cc king. Honda were really on the march.

The following year (1962) they broadened their attack, both up and down the capacity scale. Their fifty was a spindly single, appropriately ridden by the diminutive Luigi Taveri and Tommy Robb. Initially, the three-fifty was merely a two-fifty with the engine bored out to 285cc. But a full-size engine was launched in the Ulster Grand

Prix, which Redman won hands down, backed up by Tommy Robb in the 250cc event and Taveri in the 125cc.

In the Isle of Man Taveri won the Lightweight 125cc TT, but had to give best to Ernst Degner's Suzuki two-stroke in the 50cc event (as he did in the world championship, too). And though Derek Minter upset the team's plans for the Lightweight 250cc TT – by bringing home a four borrowed from the UK importers ahead of Redman's and Phillis' works jobs – it was again McIntyre who set the race alight.

A dazzling opening lap at 99·06mph put him 34·6 seconds ahead of Redman and a massive 44 seconds up on Minter. The first 250cc ton-lap was virtually in the bag for Honda and the brilliant Scot – who had been the original ton-lapper five years earlier on his Senior-winning 500cc Gilera four. Alas, half the Honda's ignition system went dead at Baaregarroo, a third of the way round the second lap.

But the season ended with Redman claim-

ing both 250 and 350cc world championships (shattering MV's four-year monopoly in the bigger class), and Taveri taking the 125cc title.

By 1963 it was clear that Honda's meteoric rise to racing fame had spurred rather than demoralised their Japanese rivals, Yamaha and Suzuki, as well as MV, the pride of Italy.

On a tremendously fast disc-valve twin that was to all intents and purposes an oriental MZ, the tearaway Fumio Ito led Redman for the first two laps of the Lightweight 250cc TT before throwing the race away by loitering over his pit stop. And in the Junior TT, Hailwood wore out a massive, specially concocted two-leading-shoe front brake in a vain bid to hold Redman. In the long run, however, physical and mechanical stamina saw Redman through to a repeat of his double world championship.

In the tiddler class, Honda had temporarily acknowledged Suzuki superiority by pulling out and scurrying back to the draw-

ing board. And a drubbing by the Suzuki one-two-five twins convinced Honda that a redesign was necessary in that class, too.

Suspecting that a disc-valve two-stroke, with tiny pots and water cooling, might ultimately have a greater power potential, Honda took the only line possible – smaller cylinders and higher peak revs.

With four pots, eight speeds and 16000 rpm, their new one-two-five dominated the TT and world championship alike. And though their 20000rpm, 50cc twin only dented Suzuki's confidence in 1964, it

robbed them of the world title in 1965.

In both years Phil Read, on the air-cooled Yamaha 250cc twin, played cat-and-mouse with Redman. The Yam lacked the stamina to win the TT, but it had speed enough for Phil to shadow Jim throughout most of the other classics, then pip him on the last lap, to give Yamaha the title.

In 1965, too, Hugh Anderson regained the 125cc championship for Suzuki, while Yamaha reinforced the two-stroke challenge in that class with a water-cooled twin good enough to win the TT. Notwithstanding

These Gooseneck shots in the 1965 Lightweight 250cc TT show that Jim Redman's six-cylinder Honda (No. 2) is no wider than Franta Stastny's single-cylinder Jawa

Top *the exhaust megaphone under the seat identifies this machine as a 125cc five*

Above *two bikes, 12 exhausts – Jim Redman leads Mike Hailwood at Hockenheim in 1966.*

Right *Mike Hailwood sets race and lap records in the 1967 Senior TT*

Redman's fourth successive world 350cc title, Honda now had their backs to the wall.

Logically enough, their answer was to push further along the small-cylinder road. The one-two-five went from four cylinders to five, the two-fifty from four to six – a masterpiece of miniaturisation in that the fairing was no wider than that of a 250cc single.

On the basis that the hand on the twist-grip is no less important than the power at the other end of the throttle wires, Mike Hailwood was snatched from MV as number one rider, and given a 500cc four into the bargain to keep him from pining.

So successful was the six that it had only to be bored out to 297cc to beat every three-fifty in sight. In 1966 Honda established a record by winning all five solo classes of the manufacturers' world championships, though two individual titles eluded them – the 50cc class falling to Hans-Georg Anscheidt (Kreidler), the 500cc to Giacomo Agostini (MV Agusta).

At the very peak of his brilliance, Hailwood made mincemeat of the following year's Lightweight 250, Junior and Senior TTs – the last after a heroic struggle with a loose twistgrip. But the two-stroke threat was still mounting ominously, as Yamaha tamed the handling of their water-cooled vee-fours and found more power.

From a purely technical viewpoint, then, Honda's withdrawal from classic racing at the end of 1967 was the greatest pity, for the final confrontation between four-stroke and two-stroke seemed imminent. As it was, Yamaha two-strokes won by default, though there were more shots in Honda's four-stroke locker. A 50cc three was already on the stocks. And who knows but what we might have seen a 125cc six, and vee-eights in the larger sizes?

Yet Honda racing design was always straightforward. Their success lay in recognising and exploiting fundamental principles. Previous European bias against four-valve heads was just that – bias. Under the post-war formula of limited capacity and no supercharging, the only way to increase power is to get the engine to breathe and burn its fill of gas more frequently.

The lighter reciprocating masses in smaller cylinders and double valves make higher revs mechanically safe. Scavenging and deep breathing are enhanced by the greater valve-opening area. Finally, combustion is improved by the more thorough turbulence of converging inlet streams, the shorter flame travel from central plugs, and the compacting of the combustion space by squish segments front and rear.

Fath Urs

Helmut Fath was a post-war throwback to the really great rider-tuners – men of courage and talent who constantly sought perfection both in their track technique and their engineering. Like all West Germany's top sidecar stars, he came to fame on a BMW outfit, showing outstanding tuning and driving ability in winning the 1960 world championship as a privateer.

A serious crash at the Nürburgring the following season put his guts to the test, too. For his comeback, which eventually took place in 1966, he planned to build the fastest BMW outfit ever. He might well have done

so but for an acute shortage of engine spares. Since they were rationed on an exchange basis and Fath had but one engine left, the extensive experiments he had in mind were out of the question. But his obsession with regaining his title was so fierce that he promptly knuckled down to the monumental task of building his own world-beater. The ultimate proof of his mettle came in 1968, when he won his second title, on his high-revving four-cylinder double-ohc Urs (the first three letters of his native Ursenbach). Meantime, his enforced switch in strategy meant that he traded the original problem

In his 1966 comeback, after five years on the sidelines following a Nürburgring crash, Helmut Fath drifts his unstreamlined Urs four round Druids Bend at Brands Hatch

of making a basically reliable outfit faster for that of making a basically fast outfit reliable.

Since the BMW layout was so beautifully tailored to sidecar racing, the only valid line of approach was more power in an equally low outfit. If the Urs engine was to give more power than the BMW – which it eventually did to the tune of 10 per cent – then it had to have more cylinders. So Fath decided on a four-abreast layout. But to a born perfectionist, nurtured on silk-smooth flat twins, a conventional four is rough.

With two pistons at top dead centre while the others are at bottom, the primary inertia forces cancel out completely. But the secondary forces (though only about a quarter the size of the primaries) act upward in unison at both dead-centre positions and downward in unison at midstroke. The net result is perfect primary balance at the cost of a secondary vibration at twice engine speed and approximately equal to the primary force from one piston.

That may be good enough for Honda, Kawasaki and MV Agusta. It was not good enough for Fath. He spaced the four crankpins at 90 degrees, like the points of a compass, so that the dead-centre and midstroke positions all coincided. Hence at the instant the primary forces from the top and bottom pistons cancelled out, their upward secondaries were balanced by downward secondaries from the two midstroke pistons.

In terms of vibration, the price of that degree of primary and secondary balance was a rocking couple. But that is the least of the various vibration evils. More serious was the effect of the crankpin layout on ignition, not just because it involved uneven firing intervals (90, 180, 270 and 180 degrees) but because, at the 14000rpm power peak, the shortest of those intervals gave only a thousandth of a second for the ignition coil to be re-energised.

Even with transistorised ignition, Fath found that the extreme right cylinder (No 4), which fired 90 degrees after the extreme left· (No 1), started to suffer from weak sparks at only 8000rpm. The solution was to fit a separate coil for each cylinder. And

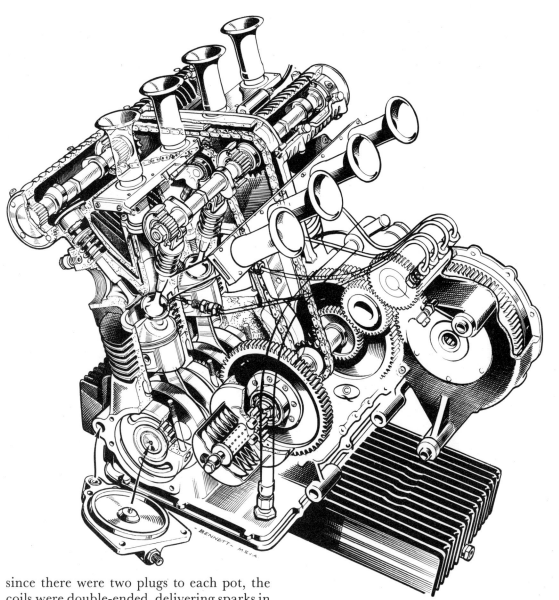

Left *the Urs engine in its 1968 world championship-winning form. The double inlet tracts converge at 60 degrees, with the injector nozzles in the floor of the lower ports. Crankpins are spaced at 90 degrees, and the shaft is in separate halves, which drive the half-speed countershaft.*

Below *throttle control (shown here with the single ports) was by a flat guillotine slide*

since there were two plugs to each pot, the coils were double-ended, delivering sparks in simultaneous pairs. But still the ignition problems were not over, for a contact breaker had to be made with four pairs of points spaced at 45, 90, 135 and 90 degrees.

Novelty in the crankshaft was not confined to the 90-degree spacing of the pins. To reduce the bending and torsional stresses in the shaft (and so permit smaller journal diameters) it was made in right and left halves, which were unconnected save in the sense that pinions in the middle of each half drove opposite ends of a half-speed countershaft. Pressed together, each half of the crankshaft incorporated four full flywheel discs, eccentrically shaped for balance. Caged needle rollers were used for the big ends and four of the six main bearings. The outer mains had crowded rollers (for their higher load-carrying capacity), their races lipped to locate the shafts endwise.

For assembly the half shafts were fed into the crankcase from below and the main bearing housings clamped up to semi-circular

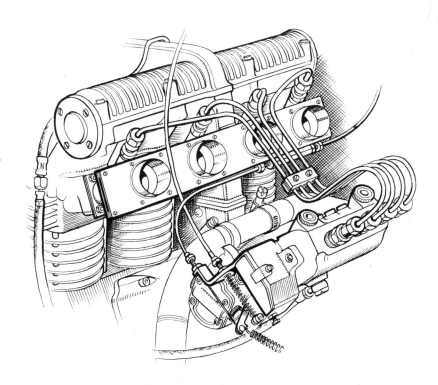

seats by two long bolts each. The pinions that drove the countershaft were just inboard of the middle bearing each side.

Made of titanium, the con rods were extraordinarily slim, with deep webs round the big-end eyes. There were only two rings on each full-skirt piston, one compression, one oil scraper. The cylinders were in light alloy with hard-chromed bores. Compression ratio was 9·3:1. The 12-stud cylinder head showed advanced thinking, with two ports converging at 60 degrees on each inlet valve. Four conventional ports had a down-draught angle of 30 degrees, so that the additional ones were parallel to the cylinder axes.

The idea was to improve cylinder filling by making fuller use of the valve periphery. But the Urs didn't get the best out of the scheme, since only the conventional ports had fuel injectors, the others passing air. Had both sets of ports been injected (or car-buretted), so that each converging airstream carried a petrol spray, the globules would have been broken up more finely, to give a more homogeneous mixture, hence more thorough combustion as well as better breathing.

It would have been difficult to find room to inject both sets of ports, however. Even as it was, the injection nozzles had to be shifted from the roof to the floor of the conventional ports when the extra ones were added. The net result was that the double-port layout did nothing to boost peak power, but improved acceleration from 11000rpm. Naturally, with port injection, the throttles were flat guillotine slides.

Though the reciprocating weight of the valve gear could have been lower – there were single, not double, valves and each

Self-made world sidecar champion in 1968, Helmut Fath lifts the sidecar wheel on a right-hander despite the acrobatics of passenger Wolfgang Kalauch

cam follower comprised a block with a needle-bearing steel roller and a hemi-spherical pad – valve float was pushed beyond 15000rpm, even with single helical springs.

The secrets here were, first, that the springs were wound from short lengths of thick ($\frac{3}{16}$in) wire, so that their natural frequency was too high for surge to set in. Second, a super-quality Swedish wire was used to withstand the higher torsional stresses in the shorter wire (only four coils per spring). Finally, the cam form was designed to suit the spring frequency. So successful were the springs that Fath soon cornered the market among his BMW rivals.

Besides the six-speed Schafleitner trans-mission, all the ancillaries were driven from the half-speed countershaft. Just inboard of the large driven gear on the right-hand end of the shaft was a pinion driving the injection pump via an idler. Outboard of the same gear was the clutch-drive pinion, giving a speed reduction of 1·8:1, hence a total primary-drive reduction of 3·6:1 from the crankshaft.

The right-hand extremity of the counter-shaft drove the contact breaker, the opposite end the oil pump. In the middle of the shaft was the chain sprocket for the drive to the camshafts. These were both made in right and left halves, clamped to opposite sides of the driven sprockets by a long waisted stud.

To lubricate the big ends, oil was fed into the outer ends of the crankshaft halves in the usual way, while the main bearings were supplied from a gallery across the front of the crankcase. But the cam-and-follower con-tacts were oiled by jets supplied from external pipes. Drain to the long, narrow, finned magnesium sump was by gravity.

Naturally, the Urs outfit didn't click right from the start. Overheating was an early problem, since the cylinders were not nearly so well placed for direct air cooling as were the BMWs. Also, the engine was prone to over-revving as the rear wheel pattered on bumps, for the flywheels had negligible inertia compared with that in a BMW. But the same pertinacity was applied to develop-ment as to design and construction.

Power of the Urs engine? Less interested in figures than in comparisons, Fath admitted that the 75 to 76bhp shown on his dyna-mometer was optimistic. But so was the 68 bhp for a top-line BMW on the same brake. The inevitable conclusion was a 10-per-cent advantage. And the proof lay in Fath's 1968 world title and another, gained by Horst Owesle on the same outfit, three years later.

Suzuki three

Throughout most of the 1960s, classic racing was vibrant with the struggle for supremacy between four-stroke and two-stroke, and it came as no real surprise when the Suzukis were the first 'strokers' to put it across the mighty Hondas in the TT and the world championships. For the East German 125cc MZ single already had the beating of the Honda twin when MZ star Ernst Degner, with the world title only a race away, defected to the west late in 1961 and joined the Hamamatsu factory.

It is true that Degner was not the brain behind the MZ design – that belonged to the brilliant and unassuming Walter Kaaden. But Degner was a first-class engineer as well as a fine rider, and he took enough know-how with him to point Suzuki in the right direction. Incidentally, his defection not only spiked MZ's title hopes, it also handed Honda the first of their many championships on a plate, with Tom Phillis as the grateful rider.

No sooner had Degner arrived at Hamamatsu than Suzuki abandoned their pathetic efforts with piston-controlled induction and

One of the most refined two-stroke roadsters ever – the Suzuki three-cylinder water-cooled GT750. There are eight rubber mountings for the engine, and the middle exhaust pipe branches into a silencer on each side

Left *a reconditioned pre-war Harley-Davidson racer with overhead inlet and side exhaust valves*

Top *revised AJS Porcupine, with inclined engine*

Centre *Mike Hailwood on a four-cylinder MV Agusta*

Above *Gunther Bartusch on an MZ twin in the 1970 Ulster GP*

fielded an MZ-type disc-valve 125cc single and 250cc twin, albeit without immediate success. They also ran a 50cc version of the single – and it was the uncanny reliability of this machine, throughout Degner's dominance of both the TT and the world championship, that first pointed up the advantages of tiny cylinders in bypassing the two-stroke's heat problems and giving more power through higher revs.

Soon, water cooling and even smaller cylinders were adopted to take both reliability and power a stage further, and Suzuki were riding high in the 50 and 125cc classes. Naturally enough, they then decided to double-up their successful one-two-five twin by tacking another pair of cylinders on the front in a much-publicised bid to push Honda off the 250cc perch, too. Incredibly for such a bold design, the Suzuki 250cc square four was the most monumental flop in post-war racing. In the smaller classes, too, the factory began to lose ground.

But they were going great guns in motocross, with Joel Robert winning the world 250cc championship first in 1964, then five years on the trot, from 1968 to 1972. During that five-year period Suzuki called on their experience of water cooling, and of porting the 70×64mm piston-induction moto-cross cylinder, to launch the three-cylinder GT750. This was easily the most exciting and luxurious two-stroke roadster ever made,

and tuned to give well over 100bhp and nudge 175mph, it practically monopolised 750cc racing from the start.

Indeed, it was with big-class racing in mind, as well as a sparkling road performance, that Suzuki chose 750cc. Settling for three cylinders not only made possible the use of some parts from the 250cc singles, but also gave very smooth high-speed running, especially with the engine mounted in rubber at eight points. Water cooling was considered essential to keep the middle cylinder happy. It also quietened the engine mechanically and enabled the cylinders to be more closely grouped than if there were deep cooling fins.

In spite of the primary-drive gears adding an inch to the space between the middle and right-hand cylinders, overall block width was kept down to 16in. To avoid cramping the area of the transfer passages in the closer-spaced middle and left cylinders, their whole port layouts were twisted 30 degrees counter-clockwise on the cylinder axes, so that the adjacent passages overlapped. Porting experience gained in motocross made for a broad spread of torque, and this was enhanced by cross-coupling of the exhaust pipes. Just behind the coupling point, the middle pipe was divided to serve a small silencer each side for symmetry.

The size of the three Mikuni carburettors was 32mm ($1\frac{1}{4}$in). And the absence of squish

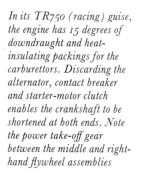

In its TR750 (racing) guise, the engine has 15 degrees of downdraught and heat-insulating packings for the carburettors. Discarding the alternator, contact breaker and starter-motor clutch enables the crankshaft to be shortened at both ends. Note the power take-off gear between the middle and right-hand flywheel assemblies

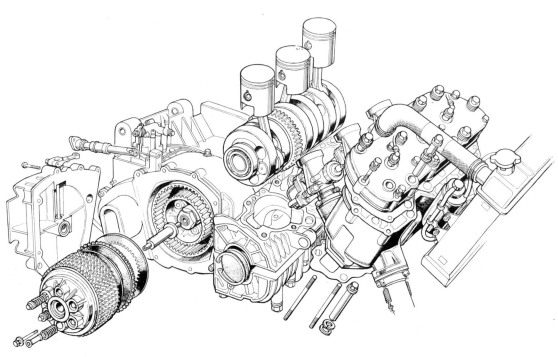

in the standard head kept the compression ratio down to 6·7:1 from exhaust-port closure (about 10:1 geometric). At the bottom end, the crankshaft was supported in four main bearings, each with a gas seal. The generator was mounted on the right-hand extremity of the shaft, the contact breaker on the other. Just inboard of the breaker was a pair of gears driving a cross-shaft behind the left-hand two flywheel assemblies. On this shaft were a worm wheel for the rev-counter drive and a skew gear for the impeller in the bottom of the crankcase.

Housed above the cross-shaft, the starter motor drove the crankshaft through double-reduction gearing and an over-run clutch

inboard of the cross-shaft gears. Transmission was five-speed all-indirect, and a worm wheel in the gearbox drove the throttle-linked Posi-Force pump that fed oil to the main bearings and inlet tracts.

Perhaps the most sophisticated feature of the GT750 was the four-stage cooling system. For rapid warming-up, the thermo-stat blanked off the outlet from the cylinder head to the radiator, and the water returned to the impeller through a bypass hose behind the block. At 82 degrees C the outlet to the radiator was opened, though some water continued to circulate via the bypass. At 95 degrees the bypass was closed and all the water went through the radiator. Should the water temperature ever reach 105 degrees, then a four-blade electric fan was automatically switched on.

Equipped so luxuriously, the GT750 stood no chance of being light – it scaled well over 500lb. But 67bhp at 6500rpm gave it 110mph and effortless high-speed cruising.

Apart from the very necessary stripping of superfluous weight, the TR750 racing version looked remarkably similar to the standard one. The most significant differences – accounting for an extra 40bhp or more – lay in the porting (allied with tuned exhaust and induction tracts) and the cylinder head.

Wide squish bands in the combustion chambers raised the compression ratio to 7.2:1 from exhaust closure (13:1 geometric), and made it necessary to dowel the head for accurate location if the piston crowns were not to foul. The middle of the divided inlet ports was deepened to extend the opening period, while the tracts themselves were shortened and given 15 degrees of down-draught. The exhaust ports were widened to the extent that they needed a bridge down the middle (to prevent ring trapping), and they were raised in the middle, again for longer opening duration.

Instead of being cast in the cylinder block, the liners were pressed in, so that all gas passages in the block could first be machined and polished. Pistons and carbs were changed for racing patterns, and ¾in-thick heat-insulating packings were sandwiched between the carb adaptors and the block. Since the alternator, contact breaker and starter clutch were discarded, the crankshaft was shortened at both ends. Uprated considerably, the clutch was run dry, instead of wet, and ventilated. Naturally, the internal gear ratios were closer spaced.

In spite of the enormous power boost and a 1500rpm increase in peak revs, the engine remained extremely torquey from 5000rpm upward, albeit petrol consumption rose to about a gallon every 15 miles. On tricky circuits Yamahas of less than half the capacity proved that a racing machine is much more than a mobile engine, but the tremendous speed and acceleration of the TR750 forced the pace of tyre development as it had not been forced for years.

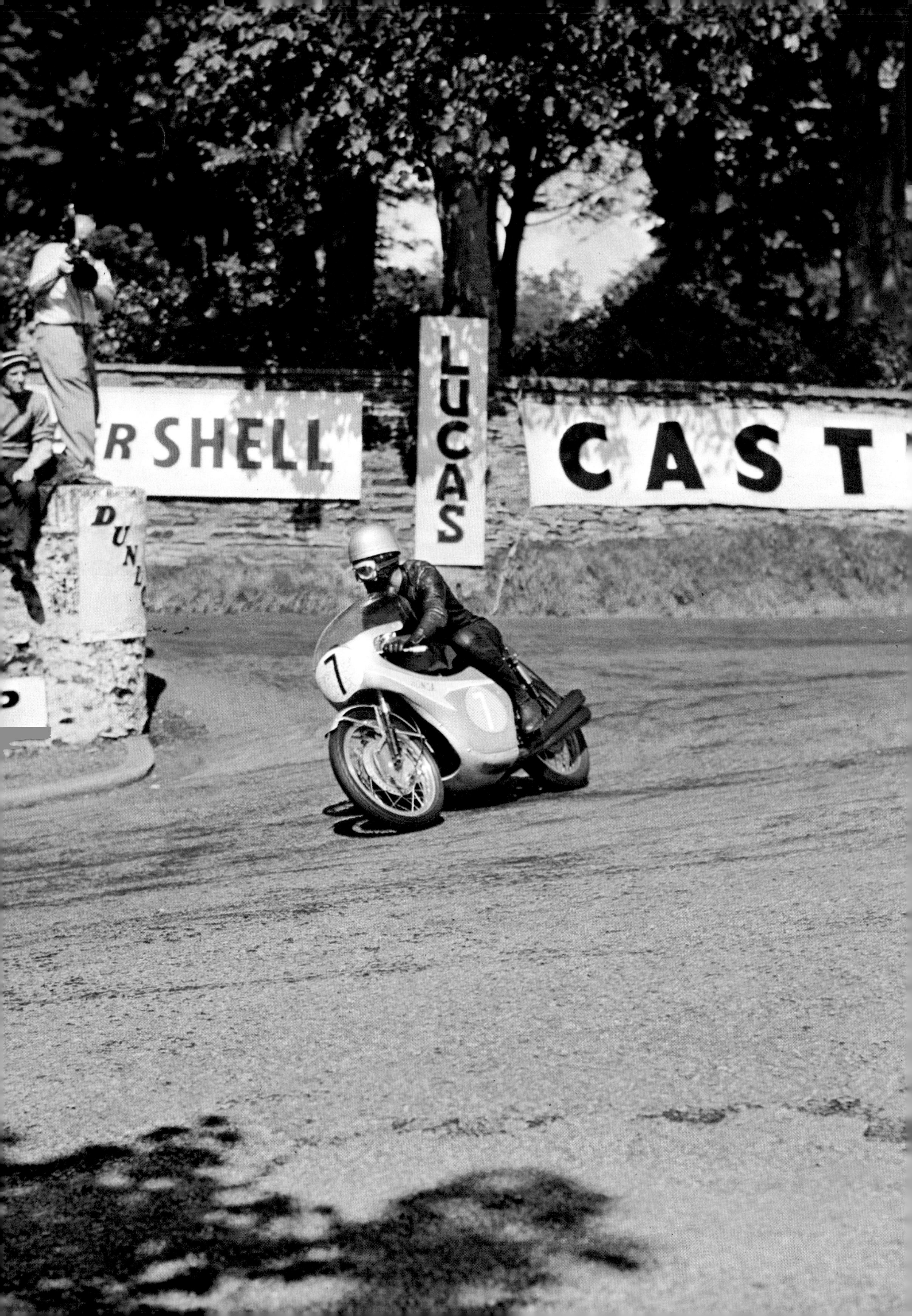
R SHELL
LUCAS
CAST
DUNL
7
1

Left *Jim Redman on a Honda four, at Governor's Bridge during his third consecutive winning Junior TT ride, in 1965*

Above *Helmut Fath and passenger Wolfgang Kalauch on the four-cylinder Urs outfit at Mallory Park*

Right *Bill Ivy at Ballaugh Bridge, setting his record lap on a Yamaha four during the 1968 250cc TT*

Yamaha vee-four

It took Yamaha eight years to fight their way up from ignominy to absolute supremacy in the Lightweight 250 and 125cc TTs, which little Bill Ivy and Phil Read won for them in 1968. Considering the dominance Honda had already established when Yamaha began, let alone the intensity of the struggle between two-stroke and four-stroke that was such a thrilling feature of classic racing throughout the 1960s, that eight years was a very brief period. Technically, Yamaha's battle was the long hard grind from a simple, air-cooled parallel-twin two-stroke in 1961 to a highly-sophisticated, water-cooled, disc-valve vee-four in 1968.

Actually they first hit the TT jackpot three years earlier, when Phil Read won the 1965 Lightweight 125cc event on a 14000-rpm water-cooled twin. But in 1968 Yamaha, despite having won three TTs on the trot (Ivy the second in 1966 and Read again in 1967), adopted the vee-four layout of the two-fifty for their smaller machine and established one of the TT's all-time milestones – the one and only ton-lap by a one-two-five. Ivy, before obeying team orders to leave the race to Read, had thrashed his 44-bhp tiddler round the 37¾-mile circuit at 100·32mph, doing a non-stop tap dance on the gear pedal to keep the revs as far as

One of the Yamaha vee-four's most sensational achievements was the only ton-lap of the Isle of Man Mountain course by a one-two-five. Here Bill Ivy heels into Cronk-ny-Mona on his 100·32mph record in 1968

possible between 17000 and 18000rpm. In winning the 250cc event four days earlier, Ivy had the satisfaction of notching a long-standing lap record in that class, too – at 105·51mph, and that from a standing start.

Peak power of the two-fifty was about 73 bhp at 14000 to 15000rpm. And though the engine's bulk made the bike look monstrous, and called for a great deal of development to tame the handling, the complexity was justi-fied. For only the previous year no less an authority than Mike Hailwood had judged 70bhp to be about the optimum power for the Mountain lap.

Not that sheer power was the sole reason for the complexity of the Yamaha fours. Indeed the swing to water cooling and smaller cylinders was dictated by the need to blend real stamina with the competitive speed they already enjoyed in their air-cooled twins. For some years the racing two-stroke had fulfilled its technical promise of superior power and speed, only to be beaten hands down for reliability. When Yamaha's intensive development programme finally cured the two-stroke's tantrums, and victory on merit seemed a valid hope, it was ironical that the battle with the four-stroke was actually won by default – as a consequence of Honda's withdrawal from classic racing at the end of 1967.

After a disappointing start in 1961 with an

Phil Read on his winning one-two-five in the 1968 East German Grand Prix

air-cooled 125cc single and a 250cc twin, Yamaha stayed at home in 1962 to search for more speed. They found it, and in 1963 Fumio Ito's new disc-valve two-fifty was phenomenally fast. Indeed, he led the ulti-mate winner, Jim Redman (Honda), for the first two laps of the Lightweight 250cc TT before throwing the race away through loitering over his pit stop. For the next two

Following pages Barry Sheene on a 750 Suzuki leads Martin Sharpe (350 Yamaha) at Mallory Park in 1974

173